Comprehension

Comprehension

Strategic Instruction
for K–3 Students

Gretchen Owocki

HEINEMANN
Portsmouth, NH

Heinemann
361 Hanover Street
Portsmouth, NH 03801–3912
www.heinemann.com

Offices and agents throughout the world

Library of Congress Cataloging-in-Publication Data
Owocki, Gretchen.
    Comprehension : strategic instruction for K–3 students / Gretchen Owocki.
        p. cm.
    Includes bibliographical references and index.
    ISBN 0-325-00576-1 (alk. paper)
    1. Reading (Early childhood).   2. Reading comprehension.   I. Title.
LB1139.5.R43O96 2003
372.47—dc21   2003007892

Editor: Lois Bridges
Production: Vicki Kasabian
Cover design: Lisa Fowler
Cover photograph: Ann Turyn/Getty Images
Typesetter: Publishers' Design and Production Services, Inc.
Manufacturing: Steve Bernier

Printed in the United States of America on acid-free paper
Sheridan 2018

For David Owocki

and

Emilia

and

in memory of Comet

1991–2001

Contents

Acknowledgments

I wish to thank my colleagues Christian Bush and Barb Huston for allowing me to conduct literacy research in their classrooms. Our work together has informed the writing of this book.

I am also grateful to my research assistant, Gabriela Marguery, for gathering the comprehension research that helped me to write this book and for thoughtfully reviewing the manuscript.

A warm thanks goes to my editor, Lois Bridges, for being an always tranquil presence across the country.

And finally, I wish to thank the graduate and undergraduate students at Saginaw Valley State University, for continually leading me to see in new ways.

Note to the Reader

If you are an early childhood teacher, you have seen children delight
at the opportunity to venture deeply into literature. As you have
shared books with them, you have seen their smiles and bearings of
engagement, heard their laughter and commentary, and listened to
their questions and expressions of wonder. As books draw children in
and take them through new worlds—through far-off galaxies, ancient
times, the traditions of modern families, or the life of a tree frog—
young readers have the opportunity to develop a passion for literature
that lasts a lifetime.

I believe that developing a passion for literature goes hand in
hand with developing strategies for meaningfully connecting with
text. *Comprehension: Strategic Instruction for K–3 Students* is a research-
informed guidebook for kindergarten through third-grade teachers
wishing to support children's passion for literature and, at the same
time, wishing to help them develop strategies for listening and reading comprehension.

In this book, you will find descriptions of the higher order comprehension strategies that are known to be used by proficient readers;
a framework for comprehension instruction that has shown to be successful in classrooms; and numerous practical ideas for helping children develop into strategic, thoughtful listeners and readers.
Throughout the chapters you will find graphic organizers, evaluation
tools, instructional charts, and examples of the kinds of language that
effective teachers use to engage students in talk about books.

While decoding and book handling are important components
of comprehending, this book's primary focus is on comprehension
macro-processes: predicting and inferring, purpose setting, retelling,
questioning, monitoring, visualizing, connecting, deciding what is

important, and evaluating. *Comprehension: Strategic Instruction for K–3 Students* provides ideas for supporting children's development of these processes through whole-class and small-group instruction, literature circles, partner reading, and independent reading.

- Chapter 1 describes the general processes in which readers and listeners engage as they make meaning from text.

- Chapter 2 describes the specific reading strategies that effective comprehenders use.

- Chapter 3 describes a framework for comprehension instruction that includes modeling, thinking aloud, guided practice, scaffolding, literature response, and observation and evaluation.

- Chapter 4 provides ideas and activities for working with each strategy in whole-class, small-group, and individualized settings.

- Chapter 5 contains ideas for supporting comprehension development through literature circles.

- Chapter 6 contains ideas for supporting comprehension development through partner reading.

- Chapter 7 provides an annotated list of literature and ideas to try with each comprehension strategy.

I hope that you come away from this book feeling freshly equipped to provide thoughtful comprehension instruction. Early childhood teachers across the country are making great strides in teaching comprehension in the ways suggested in this book, and they are finding that these practices greatly enrich children's literacy learning as well as their more general school and life experiences.

Comprehension

MAKING MEANING FROM TEXT

Kindergarten Classroom

Today we've discussed something important: sometimes, you can read the words, but that doesn't mean you know what the story means. Just figuring out what words *are* doesn't necessarily help you know what words *mean*. That's why we asked questions like, "What does that mean?" and "What does that look like?" Good readers stop as they read and ask themselves questions. We're going to practice this today when you're partner reading.

In classrooms in which children are encouraged to discuss *what* and *how* they read, teachers create a strong foundation for supporting listening and reading comprehension. The teacher in the vignette is Barb Huston. On this day, she is helping her students understand that good readers don't aimlessly plow through words and then assume that they have mastered the reading task. Instead, they are active thinkers who use all sorts of strategies to make meaning: they ask themselves questions; they pause to think; they create mental pictures; and they use personal knowledge and experiences to round out what the author has to say. In this chapter we will examine the general characteristics of effective readers and consider what early childhood teachers can do to support their development. Then, in Chapter 2, we will look more closely at the specific strategies that effective readers use.

Readers Are Active

Probably the most important characteristic of effective readers is that they are *active*. When mature readers approach a text, they put their background knowledge and experiences on high alert. Readied for action, they use all kinds of knowledge to make sense of what the author has to say. This means that they do much more than absorb the author's message; instead, they *transact* with it (Rosenblatt 1978). The term *transaction* implies that readers bring understandings and ideas to text in order to get meaning from it.

To think about how this works, take a moment to read the text in Figure 1–1. It was found by a thirty-nine-year-old male, tucked under a windshield wiper of his truck, as he was leaving work one day. After you read the piece, your task will be to think about how you used your existing knowledge to make sense of what you read.

Now that you have read the text, think about the ways in which you had to actively bring understandings to it in order to make any sense of it. For example, you probably used your knowledge of text structure to determine that it is a note, and you may have used your world knowledge to determine that it is an invitation to go fishing. Is there anything else you might determine about the message? For example, have the two parties been fishing together before? What kind of fishing relationship do you think they have? Are they competitive? Is this a playful competition? Although the author doesn't tell you

Weed Beater,

Pick a weekend:

May 25—26

June 1—2.

Fish Catcher

Figure 1–1 To Weed Beater from Fish Catcher

these things, you are probably able to figure some of them out. Good readers naturally use what they know to make sense of text.

The Fish Catcher example is intended to illustrate that to comprehend is not to simply absorb an author's meanings. Comprehending is an active process of using everything we know to construct a meaningful text, and filtering what has been written through our own knowledge and experiences. On the following pages, we will consider in more detail how this process works. Our focus will be on the ways in which readers actively use the following kinds of knowledge to make meaning from text:

- knowledge about text content
- knowledge about text structure
- pragmatic knowledge
- knowledge about the social/situational context

Readers Use Knowledge About Content

Content knowledge plays a great part in constructing meaning from text. The more individuals know about the general content of what they are reading, the deeper the meaning construction becomes. For example, if you have been fishing on a pond or small lake, you probably know that weeds are not a good thing. Weed-tangled fishing lines do not catch fish. Presumably, a weed beater is one whose line continually becomes tangled in the weeds. If you grasped that idea in Fish Catcher's note, you probably understood the text more thoroughly than someone who did not; you probably understood that Fish Catcher was poking fun at Weed Beater, and this would have told you something about their relationship. Your knowledge about content mattered.

Content knowledge makes a difference in reading all kinds of text. Simply put, when the topic is familiar, we read more easily, and we more deeply understand what we've read. For example, I have an easier time reading nonfiction material about conifer identification and bat conservation than material about investing in the stock market or identifying human diseases because conifers and bats are topics with which I am familiar. I live on a farm with thousands of conifers, many of which I have planted. I have sorted them, trimmed them, and worked to determine which species grow best in which soil conditions. Bats live on my farm, too. I have held a baby bat, buried its dead mother, and daily watched the colony depart for its evening feed. I can essentially breeze through and remember the content of even very technical material focused on these topics because they have meaning in my daily life. But, when I try to read about something like stock returns (see Figure 1–2), a topic that is of little interest to me, I

> The compound average annual nominal rate of return (including inflation) for common stocks was 10.7 percent over the period 1926–2001. This return exceeded long-term U.S. Treasury yields by over 5 percent per year. That difference was the historical equity risk premium . . . (Ibbotson 2002, 10)

Figure 1–2 The Compound Average Annual Nominal Rate of Return

throw up my arms and say, "Forget it!" The vocabulary and ideas in such material are too new to make sense to me, and soon after reading it, I forget most of what I've read. Content familiarity allows us to connect new information with what we already know and, therefore, understand and recall it more easily.

What does all of this mean for instruction? As with adults, a child's knowledge about content provides a foundation for understanding text and for building new knowledge from it. The child who has dribbled a basketball, kicked a soccer ball, thrown a football, or shot a hockey puck will more easily construct meaning from a sports-related magazine article than the child who has not. The child who has waded the shores of a pond, basked in its melodies, stroked its cattails, and caught glimpses of its blackbirds will more readily construct meaning from a pond-related poem than the child who has not. That is because the experienced child brings to the text mental images, vocabulary, and background knowledge that enhance the construction of meaning.

Therefore, content knowledge is important to consider as you evaluate children's comprehension. Text containing content familiar to the child will be easier to read, discuss, retell, and remember— things we often ask children to do to demonstrate their comprehension. When content is familiar, comprehension is going to be better.

Content knowledge is also important to consider as you provide instruction. Thinking about and discussing content before reading make it easier for children to understand text and easier for them to learn new concepts. In addition, the more background knowledge you help them build about any given topic, the easier and more memorable the reading in that area becomes. As a guiding principle, keep in mind that your comprehension instruction is just instruction until it reaches into a child's world and connects with the content-related concepts that are already developing. Only then will the readers in your classroom truly shine and show you what they can do.

Readers Use Knowledge About Structure

Readers also use their knowledge about *text structure* to construct meaning. As with content knowledge, the more knowledge children have about text structure, the easier it is to understand the author's meaning and to construct personal meanings. For example, as you began to read the Fish Catcher piece, you probably noticed right away that you were looking at a note. That is because good readers pay attention to text structure and use it to construct meaning. Knowing that it was a note helped you put together a little piece of the meaning puzzle.

Using knowledge about text structure works with all kinds of text. For example, children who are exposed to nonfiction texts such as biographies and autobiographies become familiar with the *time order* text structure. Knowledge of this structure combined with knowledge of content gives them a head start on meaning making—in fact, they are able to make predictions and inferences that connect them with the text before they even begin reading or listening to it.

The same holds true with fiction. For example, children who read traditional stories learn that authors usually introduce characters and a setting and then give the main character a problem that is eventually resolved. Often, an underlying theme is present. Such knowledge about text structure helps children predict the course of pieces and monitor their understandings as they read and listen. As children gain experience with reading a wide body of material, such as autobiographies, biographies, stories, poetry, textbooks, newspapers, magazines, and maps, they build a broad schema for text structures that helps them construct meaning from all kinds of text. Knowledge of text structure provides a mental framework for working through a text and mentally checking to see that it makes sense.

Having a schema for text structure also provides a framework for rethinking and reviewing what has been read. For example, if children know that traditional stories have characters, settings, problems, plot episodes, and resolutions, this knowledge can help them not only work forward through the content but also revisit it. They can use each of these elements of story grammar as a mental frame to guide their retelling or rethinking of what they have read. Similarly, walking back through headings in a nonfiction text such as a biography can support a reader or listener in rethinking the content.

In terms of assessment, it is important to keep in mind that children who have experience with thinking about text structure as they retell may demonstrate a more complete conceptual understanding than children who do not, *not* because they have comprehended better, but because they are using a helpful strategy for retelling. Thinking about text structure helps children to provide a complete retelling.

In terms of instruction, keep in mind that because knowledge about text structure contributes to meaning construction, it is a good idea to regularly draw students' attention to it. The best way to do this is to read with children from a variety of genres, encouraging them to attend to and discuss the way the text is organized, and also to sometimes use graphic organizers (such as story maps, time lines, and webs) to revisit text-based information. These ideas are addressed extensively in subsequent chapters.

Readers Use Pragmatic Knowledge

Another part of constructing meaning involves using *pragmatic*, or sociocultural, knowledge. When you interpreted the note from Fish Catcher, your sociocultural knowledge played a part. For example, you may have inferred that Fish Catcher is a male. You may have guessed that Weed Beater and Fish Catcher are two friends who have been fishing together before. You may have inferred that a playful competition characterizes their relationship. Every reader brings to text a set of social and cultural understandings that serves to round out what the author actually tells.

Based on our understandings and experiences in the world, we all round out text differently. Readers' interpretations of text depend on their personal backgrounds and experiences, which are shaped by the diverse familial, linguistic, religious, social, cultural, economic, and political contexts of their lives. Varied experiences lead to varied interpretations of text.

Of course, this means that we must accept varied levels of understanding and varied interpretations, but more importantly, it means that we must encourage children to recognize and put to use their sociocultural knowledge as they read. Always, children should be asking, What do I already know that will help me understand this text? How do my experiences help me read? On the affective side, children also benefit from being explicitly taught that different readers in the classroom bring different knowledge to text. No two children read or understand text in just the same way. This understanding opens doors to a conversational environment in which all children are valued for their unique knowledge and experiences.

Readers "Read" the Social/Situational Context

The *social/situational context*—the situation in which the reading occurs—is another influence on the meaning-making process. Context is shaped by a broad array of factors including the goals, stances, expectations, and pressures that surround a reading event. Let's consider how these factors influence a reader's meaning making.

First, a reader's *goals* shape the meaning that is constructed. Mature readers automatically select goals that help them meet their reading needs. For example, a reader may decide to read a novel as a way to escape and relax, or as a way to learn something about history. She may decide to read a recipe book as a way to plan a meal, or just because recipe books can be fun to browse. With each text encountered, a reader's specific goals influence the meaning that she makes by shaping what she focuses on and pays attention to.

Think for a moment about how goal setting shapes your meaning making. Let's say that while browsing at a bookstore, you decide to purchase an interesting-looking handbook on teaching spelling. In this situation, you might read differently than if you were discussing the same book with colleagues in a college course. The self-selected book could be approached more loosely. Perhaps you would scan for ideas you hadn't considered before, jotting them on a sticky note so you could remember them later. You would probably read the college course book more thoroughly, trying to purposefully remember and understand whatever you found to be new or complex so that you could discuss it with your colleagues. If you were going to be tested on the information, here would be yet another influence.

The point is that your goals determine the *stance*, or approach, you take toward reading. Your stance may fall anywhere along a continuum ranging from the *aesthetic* to the *efferent*. When you take an aesthetic stance (as with the self-selected bookstore book), you focus on making personal connections and on what you are feeling and thinking. When you take an efferent stance (as with the college book), you focus on obtaining information to carry away from the reading event (Rosenblatt 1991). The stance a reader takes influences the way she approaches the reading and, therefore, the meaning she constructs.

Now, with this in mind, think about the immense power that you wield as a teacher. As children listen and read in classrooms, they learn to pay attention to whatever helps them be successful in that setting. Teachers who continually expect children to answer only literal, fact-based questions encourage children to think at lower levels—to focus on facts and details rather than on the bigger picture. Teachers who continually insist that children take an efferent stance for reading such material as poetry and stories create readers who do not enjoy reading for the sake of reading. Teachers who pressure children to read with extremely high levels of accuracy (pronouncing each word correctly with no miscues) convince children to focus on calling words rather than on constructing meaning. Such practices violate children's natural ways of developing and stamp out their propensity to read with a sense of wonder and exploration. But teachers who have a diversity of expectations, and regularly encourage children to set their own goals and take their own stances, create flexible readers who can do all kinds of things. The *expectations* and kinds of *pressures* you (and families and communities) place on children influence the kinds of readers they become.

Readers Are Human

Of all things, we must remember that readers are human. They have moods, self-perceptions, attitudes, and interests that influence how they approach each reading event and, therefore, the meaning they construct. Part of creating a healthy literacy environment is considering these human traits of readers. Let's think about how this works.

In any classroom, there are hundreds of *moods* floating about at any given time. When it comes time to read, children may feel like playing, daydreaming, sleeping, eating, humming, talking, or screaming; and, at some of these times, they will not feel like reading or listening. When do *you* most feel like reading? Does this vary depending on the type of material you have available? Does it vary depending on what's on your mind? Depending on time of day? Many adults feel least like reading when sitting at a desk, and they aren't likely to do it when good friends are nearby to talk to. When working with children, it is always worthwhile to remember that moods influence how meaning is constructed. Children do need to learn to purposefully concentrate and to set their minds to school reading experiences, but you can show sensitivity by watching for and capitalizing on the situations in which their reading seems most focused; making comfortable areas where children can put up their feet; and teaching with a variety of material that is of interest to children. Much can be done to help children get into a mood for reading.

Self-perceptions and *attitudes* play a part in being a human reader as well. Children who see themselves as *readers* are most likely to read and most likely to develop positive attitudes toward reading. These children want to get their hands on books, and the more they do so, the more opportunities they have to develop the traits and strategies of effective readers. On the other hand, children who have come to believe that they are not good readers often develop negative attitudes toward reading. Many begin to avoid reading, go through decoding motions without attending to meaning, or say, "I don't want to do it," or "I can't." These children must be cared for with kid gloves. They must be taught that *all* children have literacy knowledge; some just have a little more experience with the kind that is valued in school settings. And, in K–3 classrooms, there is no such thing as a "not good" reader. For all children, literacy is a work in progress—something that develops over time. We expect children to develop at different rates and to demonstrate different strengths.

Negative attitudes toward reading also tend to develop when children come to believe that there is nothing in books that is of *interest* to them. Children who do not see reading as relevant to their in- and out-of-school lives often have little desire to learn to read. Why should they? If I had to learn to read with material focused on something like stock market issues, I would not be motivated either. On the other hand, children who come to see reading as connected to their lives, and who know that the purpose of reading is to encounter relevant and interesting new thoughts and ideas, want to read and want to learn to read. These children read more and work harder at making meaning; the more they read, the better they get. Feeling content and successful with reading and being interested in the material go a long way toward helping children discover the meaning-making process.

Finally, it is advantageous to work with children to consciously reflect on all of these factors—their moods, self-perceptions, attitudes, and reading interests. The more you and they become aware of these elements, the easier it will be to create an effective and humane environment for learning. For now, as you set up your environment, ask yourself if you are putting books in children's hands only so that they will be successful in future grades or only so that they will learn to decode. Or, are you also teaching reading in such a way that your students' *todays* are enriched, and their thinking expanded, by the new worlds they encounter in texts?

2

STRATEGIES FOR COMPREHENSION

First-Grade Classroom, 1968

Class, please open your books to page 21. We'll do the examples together, then you'll do three pages by yourselves. Look at the picture. What is the first sound you hear in *bug*? That's right, and what letter makes that sound? That's right. Write a *B* on the blank. Jill, I know this is easy for you, but please don't work ahead. Next picture. What is the first sound you hear in *duck*? That's right . . .

Over the years, notions of ideal early reading instruction have evolved tremendously. Traditionally, many early childhood teachers spent lots of time teaching children strategies for decoding text but little time teaching strategies for comprehending. The focus was on ensuring that children would be able to recognize and identify words and read them with an emerging fluency. Although children *were* encouraged to read actual text, the language in their readers was usually whittled down and controlled, rendering the content and structure menial. And, although children may have listened to stories read aloud, in many classrooms the readings were rarely accompanied by in-depth comprehension instruction.

Today's early childhood teachers are cognizant of the fact that although decoding is ultimately important to comprehending, learning to read requires much more than learning to decode. Today's teachers take steps to ensure that along with decoding strategies, their young students develop strategies for comprehension. In kindergarten and first-grade classrooms, a great deal of comprehension strategy instruction occurs through listening experiences; over time, children become progressively more able to apply these strategies to their independent reading.

What Are the Strategies?

Researchers in the field of reading feel confident that they have identified the most important comprehension strategies (Pressley 2001). Although different scholars categorize particular elements of the strategies in different ways, most convene on a similar set of ideas. Figure 2–1 provides a brief description of ten strategies that are commonly referred to in the professional literature as being facilitative of comprehension. You may find it helpful to photocopy this form and take it into your classroom for quick reference. Figure 2–2 provides a list of the same strategies for children to refer to. This form may be enlarged to chart size and posted on the classroom wall. On the following pages, we will examine each strategy in detail, considering the ways in which each fosters children's construction of meaning.

As you read, please keep in mind two ideas. First, most strategies operate simultaneously during any given reading event. Readers naturally use the strategies because they need them to make meaning and to achieve their reading goals. Although during lessons, you may focus on one particular strategy in order to highlight it and help your students understand it better, readers actually use most of the strategies at once. Ultimately, that is what we must help children learn to do.

Second, many studies on comprehension have occurred with older children or adults. Although researchers *have* looked at varied aspects of young children's comprehension, by no means have we finished learning about the ways in which comprehension develops in early childhood. As you continue to read about comprehension instruction, and to apply instructional techniques related to comprehension, be sure to continue learning from your students and to tailor what you do to meet *their* particular needs.

Successful Reader Strategies

Strategy	What It Involves
Predicting and Inferring	• Drawing on prior knowledge to make hypotheses (or predictions) and assumptions (or inferences) • Confirming and revising hypotheses and inferences
Purpose Setting	• Formulating goals • Taking appropriate stances • Overviewing and reading selectively to meet goals • Evaluating whether goals are achieved
Retelling	• Summarizing • Synthesizing • Rethinking • Reviewing
Questioning	• Asking who, what, when, where, why, and how questions • Asking where the answers to questions can be found • Reading selectively to find answers to questions
Monitoring	• Tracking comprehension • Revising understandings as new information is encountered • Using fix-up strategies to clarify confusions • Thinking about word meanings
Visualizing	• Mentally representing book ideas using all of the senses
Connecting	• Activating prior knowledge before, during, and after reading • Making personal connections • Making connections between texts • Considering changes in knowledge that come as a result of reading
Deciding What's Important	• Using reader purpose to determine important ideas and themes • Using text format, sequence, and features to help make decisions about what is important
Evaluating	• Critiquing and establishing opinions • Considering merit of content; considering author uses of language • Considering author intents and viewpoints • Preparing to apply new information

Figure 2–1

Strategies for Kids

Strategy	Ask yourself . . .
Predict and Infer	• What might I learn/learn next? What might happen/happen next? • What does this probably mean? • Was my prediction or inference confirmed?
Set a Purpose	• Why am I reading this book? • What do I want to get from it? • How will I meet these goals? • Have I met my goals?
Retell	• What was this text about, mainly? • What have I learned? • What is a good way to rethink this text?
Ask Questions	• What questions do I have as I read this text? • Where will I find the answers?
Monitor	• What have I just read about? • Which parts are confusing? • If parts are confusing, what fix-up strategies could I use?
Visualize	• What pictures, smells, sounds, tastes, and touches come to mind as I read this?
Connect	• What does this remind me of? • Have I seen something similar in other books? • What part of my thinking has changed after reading this?
Decide What's Important	• What are my goals? • Based on my goals, what is important? • What does the author think is important? How do I know?
Evaluate	• What do I think about this text? Why? • Why did the author write it? • How can I use this information?

Figure 2–2

Predicting and Inferring

TEACHER: [*showing the cover of a book about the solar system*] Do you think this book is fiction or nonfiction?

CHILDREN: Nonfiction . . . It has real pictures, so it looks like it's about real planets.

TEACHER: What do you think you'll learn from this book?

Predicting is a strategy that we hear about all the time, but why is it so significant to comprehending text? Why is it a recommended part of reading instruction? One central reason is that in order to predict, readers must activate their prior knowledge and use it to think about what they are about to read. In this way, predicting helps readers connect what they are reading with what they know already and bring meaning to text in order to get meaning from it (see Chapter 1).

As the example illustrates, predicting lessons often begin with children activating their thinking about *content* and *genre*. Before opening a book, teachers ask them to discuss possibilities for the content based on the title, author, and cover picture. If the book appears to be a genre of fiction, they may ask, "What do you think will happen in this story?" If it appears to be a genre of nonfiction, they may ask, "What do you know about [content of book]?" and "What do you think you'll learn?" The background knowledge used for predicting comes not only from the reader's previous experience but also from meaning that is built during the reading. Throughout a text, readers continually generate new predictions.

Effective comprehenders monitor their predictions as they read. When predictions are incorrect, they recognize this and revise their thinking. Consider the following example, in which Christian Bush uses *The Chick and the Duckling* (Ginsburg 1988) to support the prediction and revision process in her first-grade classroom. Before reading, she asks the children to "look at the pictures and think about what [the book] could be about." Based on a picture of a chick holding one end of a worm and a duckling holding the other, Amelia predicts that the book will contain a moral message "about not fighting over food." During the reading, Christian asks the children to reflect on their predictions:

AMELIA: I said that they were fighting.

CHRISTIAN: Think about the word *fighting*. Were they fighting?

AMELIA: Tugging.

To understand the story, it was important for Amelia to recognize that the creatures were indeed not fighting. In fact, they were doing something more like sharing. By helping students learn to make and revise predictions, teachers help them stay focused on the reading and guide them in using what they know so far to support the construction of new meaning.

Inferring is a strategy that is related to predicting in that it involves using background knowledge to make decisions about text. While a prediction is a smart guess about what might happen or about what might be learned, an inference is an assumption, or a supplying of information that is not explicitly stated in the text—something more like reading between the lines. When readers infer, they consider questions such as What is this character probably thinking? What might the author mean by this? and What will probably happen next? (This final question illustrates that a prediction is actually a type of inference.) As with predictions, readers revise their meaning when they find they have been incorrect.

Think about the inferring that happens just before Christian and her students read *The Lemon Drop Jar* (Widman 1991), a story about a girl whose great aunt shares a special family story:

CHRISTIAN: [*showing the cover*] What do you think this book is going to be about?

CHILDREN: A little girl and her grandma.

CHRISTIAN: Why do you think this is her grandma?

Christian's students infer that the older person on the cover is the girl's grandma "because she has gray hair" and because the child "would know better than to walk into someone *else's* house." Inferring is a strategy that compels readers to consider text in terms of their background knowledge and to create unique meanings by supplying information that is not (or not *yet*) provided by the author.

Purpose Setting

To consider the nature of the next strategy, *purpose setting*, please take a moment to walk through a simple exercise:

- Read the following nonfiction passage, entitled "The Garden Net." The passage is about a bird that becomes entangled in a net used to keep wild animals from a garden.

- Make it your purpose to track the experience of the bird. To organize your thinking, jot down *four* key experiences that you might retell to someone who hasn't read the passage.

The small dark bird became entangled in a deadly synthetic web. It wrestled, doomed to spend the close of its life as an easy target. Out of the desert sand slithered a determined assassin, moving toward the trapped bird with stealthy ease. Less than a yard separated the two, an unknowing victim and a cunning predator. A lightning strike to the head with vise-grip jaws was enough to overcome the struggling prey. The frantic flutter of small wings soon slowed to a lifeless wave. The snake turned urgently with its prize, disappearing into the thorns of the desert.

Now that you have read with a focus on the bird's experience, think about what might have happened if you had read the piece with a different purpose in mind. For example, if you had focused on the setting of the piece or the author's use of metaphor, how would the meaning you constructed have been different? Depending on your purpose, it is likely that you would have noticed different things. This exercise is intended to illustrate that a reader's purpose influences what he pays attention to and puts energy into and, therefore, the meaning that is made. Setting a purpose helps readers be efficient in their focus and achieve the specific goals they desire.

You can help children develop this strategy by first providing opportunities for them to discover that reading serves many purposes: we may read for pleasure, to find a specific piece of information, to learn how to do something, or to satisfy a curiosity. Second, regularly encourage them to set purposes as they read.

Children need to learn to set their own purposes, and even at an early age, they are very capable of doing so. Meaningful purpose setting is most likely to develop when reading occurs in meaningful contexts—in settings in which children have good *reasons* to read. For example, when Christian's students were working in groups to write fact-based scripts, purpose setting became essential. Max's group had decided to write a script about ocean creatures. Early on, the four boys set off browsing through a collection of nonfiction books and talking about all of the information. There was so much information that they struggled with what to actually write down. Eventually, they narrowed their focus to finding interesting information about sharks. The joint purpose helped them read more efficiently and develop a cohesive script.

Through this experience, Max and his peers were developing an important understanding about reading nonfiction. While stories are usually read straight through, nonfiction is usually read selectively, depending on the reader's purpose. As the group worked, they focused not on all the information, but only on pulling out interesting information about sharks: *Sharks can bite. Sharks can tip over large boats and small boats and little fishing boats. Whale sharks are the biggest sharks in the world. They weigh one hundred pounds.* Because they relied on pictures for some of their ideas, some of the information was inaccurate, but Christian wasn't worried; she was happy to see these emergent readers purposefully gathering information from several texts and working it into a single script. Other conventions could wait until later.

It is okay to sometimes set purposes for children. For example, as part of a science inquiry, you might want them to listen for the physical characteristics of insects. As part of an author study, you might want them to reflect on an author's description of various settings. Or, you may simply wish for your students to note how wonderful it is just to sit back and enjoy a good story. When *you* set the purpose, let children know exactly what it is, and model your reasoning behind it. For example, "If we focus on the body parts of these insects, we'll be able to construct accurate clay models for the science fair." Or, "Please listen carefully to this description of the setting, because it will help you understand why women did not vote in those times." Being clear with your purpose will help your students learn to focus on particular aspects of the reading and read (or listen) for particular information.

Retelling

RONNIE:	Once upon a time, Jack mama didn't have no money.
MIA:	Jack's mom told him to take the cow.
DANITRA:	He met a funny little man along the way.
FREDA:	The little man gave him some beans.
ANTOINE:	Then Jack went home to his mom. His mom threw out the beans . . .

Most young schoolchildren have opportunities to engage in *retellings* of some sort. They use puppets to dramatize *The Three Little Pigs*, costumes to reenact *Lon Po Po*, pictures to retell *The Old Woman Who Swallowed a Fly*, or voices to retell *Rumplestiltskin*. Retelling good stories is fun for children, but why is it such a valuable comprehension strategy?

The children in the vignette (Barb Huston's kindergarten students) are retelling *Jack and the Beanstalk*. To re-create the story, a flurry of comprehension activity must take place. First, each child must decide which parts are important to retell. Deciding what is important is a key part of comprehending because it focuses readers on sorting out what matters most in achieving their goals. Second, each child must listen to what has been told so far so that the retelling proceeds in a logical sequence. Sequencing helps readers rethink information in a logical order. Third, to be certain that important parts are not skipped, repeated, or misunderstood, the children must monitor their comprehension. The act of retelling brings ideas to a conscious place where children can actively monitor whether they make sense. Most important, retelling involves children in carefully thinking about and rethinking what has been read.

Retelling and rethinking are especially important for nonfiction because they help children tune in to text and understand its content better. Consider the importance of retelling and rethinking in the following example from a second-grade classroom. The teacher, Angel, is modeling her way of rethinking during reading:

> I'm going to rethink this to be sure I understand what we've read: The sap moves through the tree. If a branch breaks, sap comes out. Some saps protect the tree from insects [*closes book and looks at students*]. When I stop to retell like that, even if I don't retell out loud, it helps me to think back through what I've read and to be sure I understand it. When you are reading by yourselves, or with partners, this is a good strategy to use.

Angel is modeling a retelling strategy and, at the same time, making sure that her students understand what she is doing and why. She wants them to be consciously aware that retelling during and after reading helps readers rethink text and therefore understand it more fully.

Summarizing and *synthesizing* are terms that are directly connected with retelling; the three terms often show up together in the comprehension literature. Ellin Keene and Susan Zimmerman, in their groundbreaking book *Mosaic of Thought* (1997), make an interesting distinction between summary and synthesis. Summary is "a succinct retelling of key points in the text" (171). "Synthesis is a more personal composite of what the piece was about" (170)—more a description of the *gist* of the piece than a detailed retelling of main points. As part of retelling experiences, children should be supported in developing competencies in both summary and synthesis.

Questioning

As Barb Huston reads aloud, Jevon (her kindergarten student) pipes in with a question: "Mrs. Huston, how the lady swallowed a cow? A cow's too big."

Proficient listeners and readers are always generating *questions* as they read. They ask, What's happening here? How do these ideas fit together? Why did this happen? What are the important ideas? Questioning is an important strategy because it helps children

- move deeply into text
- think more about what they read
- organize their thinking
- frame the pursuit of new understandings
- locate specific information
- think about unstated ideas such as themes, author goals and intents, and underlying meanings

You can teach questioning by regularly drawing attention to both your students' and your own wonderings and by thinking aloud about how these may be addressed. For example, as Barb is reading aloud to her class one day, Jevon notices that the boy on the cover of the book has not yet shown up in the story. Because Jevon has listened to many books that introduce the characters right away, he raises his hand to express his wondering:

JEVON: *Mrs. Huston, why don't they got that little boy up there?*
BARB: Which one?
JEVON: That boy on the cover.
BARB: Ah, just wait. Make that your purpose, Jevon.

Barb uses this opportunity to provide a scaffold for Jevon to learn how to answer his own question. Instead of giving an answer, she suggests that he use his question to frame his thinking as he listens further. Later, she will check back with Jevon to see that his question has been answered.

In another example of questioning, Barb is reading aloud *The Seven Silly Eaters* (Hoberman 1998). In this story, the mother character becomes overwhelmed because of all the different foods she must prepare to satisfy the picky eaters in her family. As conversation ensues, Diamond generates a question that is qualitatively different from Jevon's:

SHAUN: The mom getting too tired.

DIAMOND: And she going to be a old lady. *Why can't she take them to her mama house?*

JAMAL: They'd drive the grandma crazy.

Diamond's question is different from Jevon's in a way that is important for children and teachers to understand. Jevon's question can be answered by reading further into the text. Diamond's is one whose answer requires that she *infer*, or draw information from the text and her own background knowledge (as Jamal has done in responding to her). Part of helping children become proficient questioners involves helping them learn to consider where the answers to different types of questions might be found. The Teacher Talk box offers some typical prompts that are helpful in teaching question-answer relationships.

Teacher Talk: Question-Answer Relationships

- Where could we find the answer?
- Is the answer in the text?
- Does the answer require putting together different parts of the text?
- Does the answer require you to use your background knowledge or knowledge about the world? (based on Raphael 1986)

Often, a reader's questions come in a subtle form, not necessarily being consciously articulated. But bringing questions to a conscious level is a way to be sure that children learn to get them answered. Children need to learn that when they have questions while reading, they can do something about them, and they need to learn that the answers to different kinds of questions are found in different places.

Monitoring

Seven-year-old Jay is reading aloud a report he has written about his family.

JAY: [*reading*] "My grandma reminded me of my grandma."

JAKE: That doesn't make any sense.

CAYLA: You have two grandmas?

Effective comprehenders *monitor* their comprehension as they listen to and read text. This means that they actively consider the meaning of what they are reading; when something doesn't make sense, they recognize it and either revise their thinking or use fix-up strategies to get back on track. In the example, Jake and Cayla are monitoring their understandings as they listen to Jay's reading. When something seems incomprehensible, they know they can do something about it. Monitoring requires that children have a strong *disposition for comprehension*, that they expect text to make sense and know to take action when it doesn't.

To teach monitoring, many teachers read aloud to children in whole-class settings, thinking aloud about the meaning they are constructing. When something unexpected arises, they show students how readers sometimes revise their thinking to accommodate the new information. For example, "Oh, I had thought that bats were in the bird family because they fly, but I see here that bats are really mammals." When something confusing arises, they pause to model and think aloud about ways to use fix-up strategies to get back on track. For example, "When I was reading this part, I didn't understand it, so I went back to the glossary to find *echolocation*," or "The first time I read this sentence, it didn't make sense, so I went back and reread the paragraph. Sometimes rereading can clear up a confusion." In addition to the modeling, as students read independently and in small groups, teachers support them in developing independence in using monitoring and fix-up strategies. Figure 2–3 lists ten key fix-up strategies that can be modeled and supported in early childhood classrooms.

Visualizing

Christian has just read the poem "Morning Grasses" (George 1997) to her students. Their eyes are closed as they try to visualize the scene the author has portrayed:

CHRISTIAN: Open your eyes and tell what you saw in your head.

JAKE: The grass was frozen. There was little footprints on there, but the grass came up really slow.

Visualizing is a strategy that children use to transport themselves into the worlds of texts. When children visualize, they make pictures in their heads, or create mental images and contexts that are an interlacing of what they have heard or read and what they have experienced in the world. Visualizing involves mentally imagining not only the *sights* but also the *sounds*, *smells*, *tastes*, *physical sensations*, and *emotions* evoked

Fix-Up Strategies

When I get confused, I can . . .

- Reread to see if the confusion is clarified.

- Read on to see if the confusion is clarified.

- Read the confusing part aloud.

- Read more slowly.

- Check punctuation to see if that clarifies.

- Look carefully at the illustrations.

- Think about whether the text structure or format gives any clues.

- Identify any confusing words. Does the surrounding text help? Is this a creative or figurative use of language? Look for a definition somewhere in the book.

- Talk out the confusion with a friend. Retell the main points and try to identify the specific confusion. Consider whether my purpose will be met if I move on.

- Ask someone for help.

Figure 2–3

by a reading (Keene and Zimmerman 1997). Consider the language Christian uses in supporting this broad view of visualization: "Keep your eyes closed and look around you. What do you see? Think about what you see . . . smell . . . hear . . . if you feel anything." Christian's cues are aimed at helping her students learn to take the time to experience and fully live through the text. Visualization is an important strategy because it helps readers and listeners round out what the author has to say and deeply experience it from their own perspectives.

To get a feel for how *you* use visualization, read the following passage from *Why Frogs Are Wet* (Hawes 1968, 28–29) and take the time to visualize what is happening. Remember that visualization involves using all of the senses.

> A frog's tongue is different from ours. It is attached to the front of its mouth. It folds back toward its throat. As a frog jumps for an insect, its tongue flips forward. The far end of the tongue has a sticky surface. This sticky end wraps around the insect. The insect sticks to the tongue, and the tongue swings back into the frog's mouth. The frog throws the insect down its throat. All this takes less than a tenth of a second.

When I read this passage with students, we talk about what we would see, hear, and feel if we could have a close-up view of this event. We use movement, too: we curl up an arm to represent a frog's tongue and then flip it forward to wrap around the insect before tossing it back down our throats. Such mental and physical activity helps children create a visual, moving picture of what has been read and therefore understand it more thoroughly.

Connecting

Connecting is a strategy that involves making (1) personal connections with texts and (2) connections between texts. Connections may happen before, during, and after reading.

Personal Connections

Personal connections happen when readers link their own knowledge, understandings, and experiences with what they read—and use this linking to construct meaning. When Christian read her students *The Lemon Drop Jar* (Widman 1992), she knew from experience that many of them would make some interesting personal connections. In this story, a young girl visits her Great Aunt Emma, who tells of the special significance behind a treasured lemon drop jar. After reading,

Christian and the children discussed different family traditions that people around the country and world have and also the traditions that the children had experienced in their own lives. Christian told the students that to enrich their understandings of the piece, they could write about any personal connections they had made. After discussing and writing about their ideas, Samantha and Cayla told the children in their literature circles about their connections:

> SAMANTHA: A very, very long time ago, I went to my Aunt Jeanette's. She gave me a [glass] rabbit to play with. My mom put it up very high. I climbed up on my chair and got it down and nothing broke. My mom said to put it back. Then, when I was older, my brother asked to see it and I started crying because I was the one who did it with my Aunt Jeanette.

> CAYLA: My grandpa died, and when I see his picture, it reminds me of when he always gave me one dollar every time I go to his house.

Personal connections enhance children's understandings of text by helping them relate to events and settings and tuning them in to the joys and tensions of characters. By supporting children in making personal connections, we help them more deeply understand what they read.

Connections Between Texts

Connections between texts happen when children make associations between any two pieces of written language—and use these associations to build their overall schema for the world. Throughout the year, with *The Lemon Drop Jar* and other books (fiction and nonfiction), Christian's students explored connections *between* texts as well. By exploring connections between a number of books about families, the children gained a strong sense of what makes a family, what families do together, the different traditions that families share, and so on. In this way, focusing on connections between texts enabled them to develop their schema, or worldview, for the concept of family.

In fact, the students learned about many topics with the help of making connections between texts. They read a number of texts about insects, animals, friendship, and famous people. They studied different genres this way, too, such as stories, poetry, autobiographies, and biographies. Teachers support their students in developing their schemas for all kinds of things by supporting their between-text connections.

Deciding What's Important

Deciding what's important is our next strategy. Books contain many interesting things for children to pay attention to—captivating illustrations, interesting words, funny characters, suspenseful story lines, remarkable human feats, fascinating facts, and so on—but there are times when a reader has a specific purpose in mind, and paying attention to certain ideas or points (rather than those that seem most interesting at the moment) is beneficial. For example, in the earlier example from Christian's classroom, Max and his peers were seeking interesting information about sharks, but the books also contained information about numerous other aquatic creatures. In that scenario, the children were successful because they developed a strategy for narrowing their focus to what was important in reaching their goals.

How does deciding what's important work? First, readers' *goals* and *purposes* always influence their decisions about what is important. Max's group's goal was to present interesting facts about sharks. This determined the focus of the children's reading. If their goal had been, say, to present interesting real-life stories about sharks, they would have focused their attention differently.

Text *structure* helps children decide what's important, too. When deciding what is important in stories, for example, young children learn to draw from their familiarity with typical story features. They may look for the beginning, middle, and ending; the major plot episodes; or the characters, setting, problem, and resolution. Thinking about story structure helps them think about what's important. In deciding what is important with nonfiction, readers use different text structures. Nonfiction is often organized in terms of description, cause and effect, comparison, time order, or problem resolution. Figure 2–4 shows some graphic organizers that support children in organizing ideas from nonfiction. With guidance, young children can use these structures to help sort out the most important ideas.

Finally, examining text *features* helps children make decisions about what is important. For example, authors often signal importance with headings, fonts, graphics, illustrations, summary statements, marginal notes, and cue words (such as *first, next, in conclusion*, and *most important*). When children learn strategies for deciding what's important, their reading becomes focused and efficient.

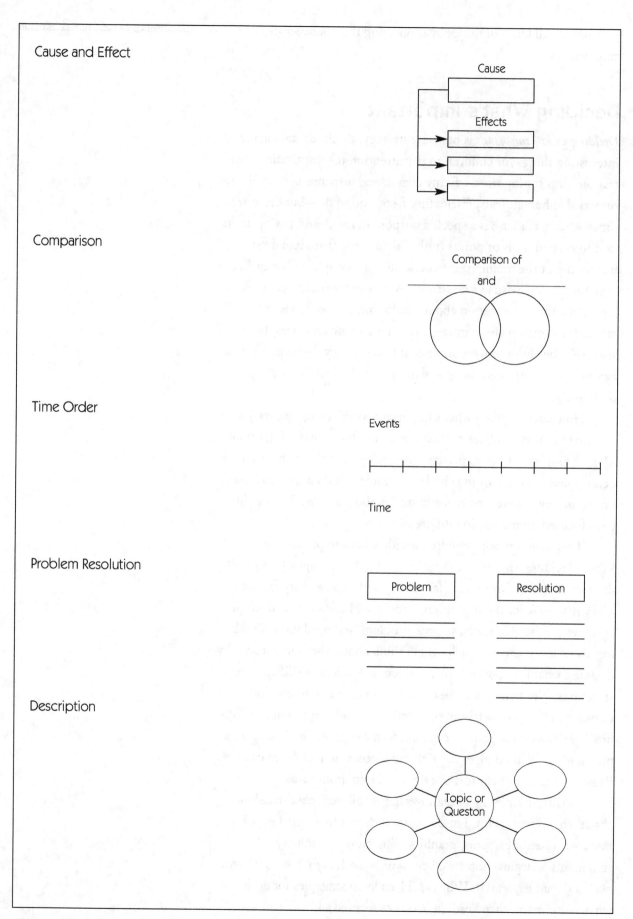

Cause and Effect

Cause

Effects

Comparison

Comparison of

_____ and _____

Time Order

Events

Time

Problem Resolution

| Problem | Resolution |

Description

Topic or
Queston

Figure 2–4   Graphic Organizers for Nonfiction

Evaluating

Evaluating is our final strategy. Evaluating involves all kinds of cognitive activities, including the following:

- critiquing
- establishing opinions
- considering author intents and viewpoints
- preparing to use and apply new information gained from reading

Because of the broad nature of this strategy, a series of questions to discuss with and model for students will offer the most efficient way to describe it. The Teacher Talk box provides examples.

Teacher Talk: Evaluating Text

- What do you think about this piece? Why? What makes you like it/not like it?
- What do you think of the illustrations? How do they help you understand this text?
- Why do you think the author wrote this? Who should read this? Why?
- What do we know about the author? Do you think that being (in a wheelchair, a woman, Native American) makes a difference in what this author has to say?
- Do you agree with this author's views?
- Are people from parallel cultures (boys and girls, men and women, people of color) presented realistically or in stereotypical roles?
- Fiction: Do the characters seem real? Is this how (kids, adults, grandmothers) really act/sound? Could this really happen?
- Nonfiction: Is this easy to understand? Why? Does it make sense? Why? What do you think of the examples?
- How can you use this information?
- What do you think of the way the author uses language (such as imagery, alliteration, or rhyme)?

As you can see, evaluation encompasses a diverse range of thinking. As with all of the strategies, the best ways to teach evaluation are to highlight and support student uses of the strategy and to model and think aloud about your own uses as they become relevant to your meaning making.

3

A Framework for Comprehension Instruction

Third-Grade Classroom

Monica is a third-grade teacher whose students have been participating in literature discussion groups. Patrick's group has just finished reading *Titanic* (Sherrow 2001).

MONICA:	What did you think about this book, Patrick?
PATRICK:	It was good.
MONICA:	What was good about it?
PATRICK:	The pictures helped us learn about the Titanic and how big it was . . .

The goals of comprehension instruction are to ensure that children engage with, deeply reflect on, and learn from what they read. In Chapter 2, we examined a set of comprehension strategies that the professional literature suggests will help children meet these goals. Along with convening on a set of comprehension strategies, the professional literature convenes on a set of techniques found to be helpful in teaching these strategies. These teaching techniques include

- creating a learning environment that fosters dispositions for comprehension
- teacher modeling and thinking aloud about strategy use
- providing time for independent, partner, and guided reading
- scaffolding children's use of reading strategies
- supporting varied forms of literature response
- observing, documenting, and evaluating children's reading and listening capabilities

Within an instructional setting that incorporates these techniques, children have numerous and diverse opportunities to develop the comprehension strategies that are essential for proficient reading. We turn next to a close look at each technique.

Fostering Dispositions for Comprehension

For all young children, successful meaning making begins with developing a *disposition for comprehension:* an expectation that text will make sense that is accompanied by a propensity to use meaning-making strategies. A disposition for comprehension is important because it is what internally stimulates children to tune in to the meaning of text and to thoughtfully consider its connections to their worlds.

Involve Children with Engaging Text

Teachers foster dispositions for comprehension by first ensuring that their students want to engage with text. If we want children to actively seek meaning from text, we must ensure that the materials are meaningful to them. Whether you or your students select the materials for comprehension instruction (some of both is good), it is important that they find the materials interesting and worth talking about. Storybooks, informational books, textbooks, newspapers, magazines, and Web-based information are good choices for comprehension instruction because they offer a variety of topics and genres to appeal to a variety of children—and because children need to learn to use all of these materials. Simple, one-sentence-per-page texts do not work well for comprehension instruction because they provide few opportunities for connecting, visualizing, questioning, purpose setting, and the like. Fostering engagement with text is a key to fostering dispositions for comprehension.

Help Children Connect Known with New Literacies

Another part of fostering dispositions for comprehension involves helping children connect school literacies with their familiar home literacies. We know that literacy is a sociocultural practice; it is used as a part of children's everyday lives. Students' families may read informational books and instruction manuals; Web documents and email; recipe books and food packages; religious materials; and more. Every child comes to school with some literacy experience. With a little effort, teachers can capitalize on this experience in the school setting.

What literacy materials are familiar to your students? In what languages are these materials written? What kinds of materials could your students bring in to be used for sharing, demonstrations, and instruction? Could they bring a book; a manual; a piece of mail; a favorite cereal box; a document printed from the Internet; a note from a family member; a comic strip; or a short newspaper or magazine column? All of these materials may be used to teach comprehension strategies.

There is no question that school is a place to *expand* literacy knowledge, interests, and practices, but when school literacy is too far separated from children's home lives and interests, many have difficulty making connections between instruction, reading, and writing. Figure 3–1 offers an example of a survey that one teacher created in order to collect a meaningful set of materials for instruction.

Engage Children in Thoughtful, Authentic Reading

Another key to fostering dispositions for comprehension is to ensure that the reading your students do at school is purposeful and meaningful. With the best kinds of instruction, children don't just learn to read words or just learn to use strategies; they learn to read all kinds of texts, *in thoughtful ways*, based on what they want to accomplish and what they want to know. For example, when Barb Huston's inner-city kindergarten students became frustrated with the litter on their school playground, they decided to do something about it. They knew that to make an impact, they would need to develop expertise on the issue, so they started asking questions: Why is litter bad for the environment? What can people do about pollution? Why do people litter on our playground? Barb and the students used *questioning* as a strategy to gather information from books and from the people who used their playground.

Barb's focus was not on teaching the strategy per se, but on teaching her students to use it to meet a real-life goal. Teaching questioning is a part of Barb's year-to-year practice, but she waited until it seemed particularly relevant to emphasize it. She taught questioning when she did because it supported her students' real-life work in the classroom and was a way for them to collaborate socially on a project they all cared about. "Socially shared intellectual work that is organised around joint accomplishment of tasks . . . allows elements of whatever skills are involved to take on meaning in the context of the whole" (Cambourne 2002, 760). The strategy of questioning took on meaning as a way to accomplish a goal that the children valued.

Barb's example illustrates that children do not need to wait until they can fluently decode in order to read thoughtfully or read to learn. Even very young children can read (and learn to use strategies) in ways that are relevant to their lives, their questions, their curriculum,

Information Request for Families

Dear _____ ,

Children have an easier time learning to read when they use materials that connect with their interests and experiences. Please get together with your child to respond to the items below. I will use the information to collect reading materials for the classroom.

1. Name three things your child likes to do.

2. Name three topics you think your child would be interested in reading about at school.

3. For the months of _____ and _____, we will be taking a little time each day to read materials that the children bring from home. I would appreciate it if you could please send one of the following items: a storybook, an informational book, a recipe book, a favorite cereal box, a printout from a website, a note from a family member, a greeting card, a comic strip, a short newspaper or magazine article, an advertisement, a coupon, or anything else along these lines! Materials written in languages other than English are welcome. Please name the item that you and your child have selected and send it to school as soon as possible:

_____

Thank you for your time and support. All items will be returned within two months.

Sincerely,

_____

Figure 3–1

and their worlds. In-depth projects go a long way toward supporting such learning. Long projects that integrate subjects and carry across several days, as opposed to shorter reading and response tasks, have been found to lead to more effective literacy learning (Allington 2002). It is in authentic, in-depth reading situations that children develop dispositions for comprehension and the strategies they need to support those dispositions.

Teacher Modeling and Thinking Aloud

As they support children in developing dispositions for comprehension, effective teachers make intentional efforts to support their development of numerous comprehension strategies. Successful comprehenders have more strategies available and are more likely to use them than unsuccessful comprehenders (Walczyk 2000). Along with having more strategies, successful comprehenders are more consciously (metacognitively) aware of them and use them more purposefully. The question then becomes: How can we help students develop strategies *and at the same time* become consciously aware of how they work?

The professional literature suggests that a key way is to *model* your uses of strategies while *thinking aloud* about how and why you are using them. "If our goal is to help students become strategic and thoughtful readers, then we must make clear to students what skillful readers do" (Villaume and Brabham 2002, 672). For example, if children are expected to retell a story, it helps to show them *and* talk them through how this is done. If children are expected to apply information from informational texts, it helps to demonstrate the process *and* make explicit the kinds of strategies that you use to do so. If children are expected to answer comprehension questions, it helps to demonstrate how you answer questions *and* make clear the strategies you use to do this. Given time to read, children independently develop many of their own strategies, but teachers facilitate their efforts by supporting them with an adult perspective that makes strategic processes explicit.

The term *explicit* is frequently used to describe the kind of comprehension instruction that focuses on the direct teaching of strategies and on making visible the often covert processes of effective readers. However, explicitness can be interpreted in many ways and can therefore influence instruction in many ways. Explicitness works best when it connects significantly with learners and takes its shape in response to what they are doing and thinking. "Useful explicitness in teaching involves selecting from all the things one could teach by thinking about the learner. . . . Explicitness, then, is not a feature of the teaching itself, but is a feature of the transaction between teaching, the learner, and the material to be learned" (Bomer 1998, 11–12). As you plan and teach, keep in mind that *your* modeling efforts must be responsive to *your students'* reading and listening needs.

Figure 3–2 provides a general outline for a whole-class or small-group lesson that is characterized by explicit teaching. The focus of the lesson is on deciding what's important.

As you model comprehension processes and think aloud about their uses, it is important to make clear to your students that readers use each strategy for a *variety* of different purposes. For example, deciding what's important could be used to collect information for a class project (as in the lesson example), or it could be used as a more general monitoring process in which a reader asks, Have I noted the important ideas? Retelling could be used to help think through key ideas, to entertain, to share information, or as a tool for readers to double-check that they have understood the content. We use strategies because they serve actual purposes in our reading and in our lives; each strategy can be useful in many ways.

Providing Time for Reading

Probably the most important component of comprehension instruction is to provide time for children to read—independently, with partners, and in guided reading groups. Effective teachers have faith in children as learners. They trust that their actual reading (both with and without the presence of an adult) is an important context for strategy development. Therefore, you should ask yourself three important questions:

- What percentage of the day do my students actually spend reading?
- What percentage of time in the literacy block do they actually spend reading?
- What does my classroom library look like?

Teachers who are the most effective in supporting children's literacy have been found to devote more time to guided and independent reading (including in the content areas) than teachers who are less effective (Allington 2002). And, in classrooms that have libraries, children read 50 percent more books than children in classrooms without libraries (Cullinan and Galda 1998).

Some of the books that you provide for children to read *independently* and *with partners* should be relatively easy to read. Easy reading

Lesson Plan: Deciding What's Important

1. **Introduce the literature by discussing the title, author, and cover illustration.** Let's think about all the information provided by the cover of this book . . .

2. **Set the purpose.** My goal is to read this book to learn more about baby dolphins. I'm going to add what I learn to the Baby Dolphins section of our web. Remember that we're going to use this web to make our class book about dolphins.

3. **Activate thinking about the topic and genre.** Do you think this book is fiction or nonfiction? Looking through the pictures and headings, what do you think we'll learn?

4. **Tell the children what strategy you will be modeling, and make clear how that strategy could be useful to them.** Today I want to talk with you about an important strategy that readers use: *deciding what's important.* One way readers decide what's important is to think about their goals. This book is about all kinds of sea creatures, but my goal is to learn just about baby dolphins. For me, what's important will be the information about baby dolphins. When I was turning through the pages, I saw that there was a heading titled "Babies." See how focusing on what's important helps me read just the information I need? Instead of reading the whole book, I'm going to start with this section.

5. **Read the literature to or with students, discussing the content as appropriate. As you read, model your way of using the strategy, and think aloud about how you are using it.** As I read, I can see that I'll need to use the strategy of deciding what's important again. The "Babies" section includes information on all kinds of sea babies, not just dolphins. I'll probably need to read through all of this, but since I need information just on baby dolphins, I'm going to focus on that and record only that information on the web.

6. **Engage with children in a discussion about what you have read or learned and how the strategy supported your meaning making.** Now, this web helps me see what I've learned about baby dolphins. I've learned . . . Using my goal to decide what was important helped me to read smartly. Instead of reading the whole book, I read just the section on babies. Instead of focusing on all sea babies, I just focused on dolphins.

7. **Arrange for children to engage in some sort of response to the literature and/or to do some further reading or listening that will allow them to more independently work with the strategy.**

Figure 3–2 Lesson Plan

allows children to gain experience with meaning making instead of putting an excessive amount of effort into decoding. All of your students, even those who need extra support, should have access to a variety of books that they can read and make meaning from successfully. In early childhood classrooms, this means having available wordless picture books, big books that have been read aloud several times, familiar storybooks, and nonfiction books with appealing pictures that help guide retellings. Don't limit your students to easy reading or simple content, though. More difficult material gives children opportunities to challenge themselves and to work out for themselves how to solve the tough comprehension problems.

In general, material for *guided reading* groups can be more challenging because this is when you are most available to read with students and scaffold the type of strategy use that will enable them to be successful. During this time, you are also available to support the children in discussing and responding to the literature. Often, books used for guided reading are later used for independent and partner reading.

Scaffolding

Scaffolding (Wood, Bruner, and Ross 1976) is another component of effective comprehension instruction. Scaffolding refers to a style of interacting that is likely to move children to a point of thinking that is just beyond where they could go on their own. Achieving this point is important because what children can do with guidance today, they are able to do on their own tomorrow (Vygotsky 1978). Giving your students plenty of opportunities to engage in real acts of listening and reading gives you plenty of opportunities to scaffold. As your students work their way through books and responses to literature, your role as a scaffolder is to take note of their understandings and to provide strategy support that will take them just a step further than they could go on their own.

It is important that teachers have a good understanding of how to scaffold, because it has shown time and again to be highly supportive of children's learning (Berk and Winsler 1995). However, the term has come to be used rather loosely; some educators use it to describe almost *any* kind of teaching interaction. Unfortunately, this detracts from its strength as a metaphor to guide effective teaching. A wide body of literature shows that effective scaffolding has the following characteristics:

- *Joint problem solving.* The child engages collaboratively with an adult (or another child) to reach a goal. (A child and a teacher are involved in comprehending a book together.)

- *Intersubjectivity*. Each partner in the activity strives for a shared view and adjusts to the perspective of the other. (The child and the teacher each come to understand the meaning the other is constructing.)

- *Warmth and responsiveness*. The expert partner stays in tune with the child's thinking, warmly providing just enough support for the goal to be reached. (The teacher observes what the child knows and can do, enabling the provision of strategic support that leads the child toward deeper comprehension.)

- *Challenging but achievable tasks*. Tasks are structured to be challenging but achievable, with the expert adjusting the amount of support to keep activities within this realm. (The material is challenging enough to require support; comprehension is achievable through thoughtful interactions.)

- *Promotion of self-regulation*. The child maintains as much control and responsibility for the task as possible. (The adult allows the child to control as much of the reading and discussion as possible.) (Berk and Winsler 1995)

To scaffold effectively requires that you pay close attention to the way you use talk in your instruction. Effective literacy scaffolding encourages *conversational talk*, in which teachers and students discuss "ideas, concepts, hypotheses, strategies, and responses with one another" (Allington 2002, 744). This means that rather than taking the lead or doing most of the talking during conversations, you allow your students to share their thinking and you participate as a member with important perspectives to share.

However, a different pattern of talk, *interrogational talk*, has been documented to predominate in classrooms. Interrogational talk is characterized by a teacher posing questions, followed by a student response, followed by teacher verification or correction (Allington 2002). The following example illustrates:

TEACHER: Amy, where did the bear go first?

AMY: To the stream.

TEACHER: Not to the stream . . . Kim, do you know where she went first?

KIM: To the tree stump?

TEACHER: Good. To the tree stump. Why did she go there?

The problem with interrogational talk is that it leaves little room for conversation or deep thinking among children. Instead of working to build literacy understandings *with* students by drawing from what they say and do, the teacher controls the conversation, often in ways that are irrelevant to the children's thinking. Effective scaffolders teach from behind. They let children's ideas direct the conversation and provide the adult perspective as it becomes relevant.

Effective teachers have also been found to ask more open-ended questions (Allington 2002). Open-ended questions allow for numerous possible responses and therefore keep conversations going. They allow teachers to examine children's thinking, and use of strategies, rather than setting children's ideas up only to be verified or corrected. When you next get the chance, ask a colleague or parent to document all of the questions that you and your children ask and answer for thirty minutes or so during reading instruction. Who asks the questions? Do you use open-ended questions? Do you scaffold? Do you interrogate? The results are sure to be interesting and informative.

Encouraging Types of Literature Response

Considering that the major goal of comprehension instruction is to encourage children to actively engage with text, *literature response* is an important part of the curriculum. *Response* is any kind of thinking or activity that involves children in taking a closer look at, or thinking again about, text. Four types of response are typical in early childhood classrooms: visual, written, dramatic, and oral.

Visual response includes activities such as drawing, painting, modeling, sculpting, visualizing, and retelling with props. Visual response provides children with "opportunities to communicate what they are thinking at any stage of knowing. Before they can . . . write [conventional symbols,] children are encouraged to express their understandings in symbolic languages they *can* use" (Houck 1997, 33–34). Visual response becomes especially important for second language learners. Children may be encouraged to tell in drawings what they cannot yet express orally or in writing. Since building comprehension is an important part of oral and written language acquisition, this is a highly recommended practice.

Written response includes activities such as writing about personal connections, creating maps for retelling, jotting down questions, listing important ideas, and writing evaluations and critiques. Written response compels children to revisit text and to conceptualize their ideas and understandings in new ways. Like visual response, written response is a way for children to develop their thinking.

Dramatic response includes activities such as reenacting scenes and performing puppet shows. Dramatic response is another way of knowing. As children contextualize what they have read for a new audience, and present it through their own language, they see it in new ways.

Oral response involves any kind of talk about text. All comprehension strategies are explored through oral response. Oral response allows children to articulate impressions, clarify for themselves (and you) what they have understood, and use others' interpretations and ideas to build their knowledge.

Responding to literature is a necessary part of comprehension instruction; it challenges children to rethink and revisit what they have read and enhances the experience of learning through written language.

Observing, Documenting, and Evaluating

Observation and *documentation* are two more key components of effective comprehension instruction. In order to effectively scaffold, you must observe and document (1) children's conceptual understandings of text, (2) their use of comprehension strategies, and (3) their growth in these two areas. This is primarily accomplished through taking anecdotal notes and collecting work samples. Anecdotal notes are brief written phrases that help teachers remember and reflect on children's demonstrated competencies and needs. Work samples are any written or drawn responses to literature and may be in the form of journals, webs, maps, and other similar items. A complete collection of materials to document a child's reading and listening competencies might include the following:

- anecdotal notes from individual, small-group, and/or partner reading, retellings, and discussions (Focus the notes on children's conceptual understandings as well as their uses of strategies for constructing meaning.)

- work samples (journals, webs, maps, drawings)

- written, taped, or drawn retellings from fiction and nonfiction

- miscue analysis (for information on miscue procedures, see Wilde 2000 or Owocki and Goodman 2002) or running records

- log of books read that includes information about the topic, author, and genre (see Figure 3–3)

- list of student's stated preferences regarding topics and genres

- statement of reading strengths constructed by student and teacher

- statement of reading goals mutually decided upon by student and teacher and, when possible, an adult family member

Books I Have Read in the Month of _____

Title	Topic	Author	Genre	Date

Figure 3–3

Try keeping the notes and materials you collect in a loose-leaf comprehension work folder with enough room for each child. That way, you can easily refer back to it for both individual and group planning. Developing a set of questions (see Figure 3–4) can help you organize your data gathering. The questions you develop should be directly aimed at tailoring your instruction to meet your students' needs. As you observe, your overarching question is not, Are they learning these strategies? but How are their uses of strategies enhancing their meaning making?

With practice, you will find that observation and documentation serve very useful purposes in planning instruction. Rather than choosing strategies and instructional techniques well ahead of time, your observations enable you to teach in ways that are relevant to the children's progress and activity. With this type of instruction, optimal learning occurs.

To begin, choose two or three of the comprehension strategies that you feel would be most useful to work on with your students. Focus your whole-class lessons on one strategy at a time and encourage your students to use this strategy during independent and small-group reading. (It may take up to a month or two for your students to become comfortable with using some of the strategies.) As you teach, you will notice that not just one but many strategies are actually used during any reading event. Go ahead and discuss other strategies as they are relevant, because good readers use many, but at times try to keep children's attention on the focus strategy long enough for them to learn to use it well. As children discuss and try out the strategies, take note of both individual and whole-class successes and struggles. Ask children questions about their ways of making meaning. Let children know that your note taking is focused on documenting their strengths and needs.

From here, you will get a good feel for how to expand and develop your instruction. Continue to work with the whole class. Form need-based groups, as different children will benefit from them, but be sure to invite "experts" to these groups, so that children have the experience of modeling for and learning from each other. Use guided reading groups (teacher-led groups that meet two to three times per week) to ensure that all of your students have opportunities to receive your support on comprehension. Typically, early childhood teachers focus guided reading instruction on decoding, but children need individualized support with both decoding and comprehension. Continue to encourage individual and partner reading, engaging in over-the-shoulder conferences that support children in talking about the content of what they are reading and also about their strategy use.

Questions for Individual and Small-Group Evaluation

- **Predicting:** What do you think will happen/happen next? What do you think you will learn/learn next? Are your predictions confirmed? *(Document the child's ability to make logical predictions and to confirm/disconfirm as appropriate.)*

- **Inferring:** Why did this probably happen? What will probably happen? What is this character/personality probably thinking? Why do you think the character/personality probably did this? What can you infer from this illustration? What did the author mean by _____? What was the author probably thinking? *(Document the child's ability to draw conclusions not explicitly stated in the text.)*

- **Purpose Setting:** Why did you choose to read this? What information are you focusing on? *(Document whether the child is setting purposes and following through.)*

- **Retelling:** What did you read about? *(Document how well the child has understood the text. Brief notes from a retelling, summary, or synthesis are all that is needed. Consider whether key story elements or key concepts from informational text are included.)*

- **Questioning:** What did you wonder about? *(Document whether the child is asking questions. Document the kinds of questions the child is asking.)*

- **Monitoring:** Did you understand what you read? Tell me a little about what you read. Did you find any parts confusing? What did you do when you were confused? How can I help? *(Document whether the child is aware of/using self-monitoring strategies and fix-up strategies. Which strategies would be useful to work on further?)*

- **Visualizing:** What did you picture in your mind as you read? What other senses could help you understand what you've read? *(Document evidence of visualization.)*

- **Connecting:** What did this make you think about? *(Document the kinds of personal and between-text connections the child is making.)*

- **Deciding What's Important:** What were your goals as you read? What did you think was most important? What do you think the author thought was most important? *(Document the extent to which the child is able to decide what is important in light of his or her goals. Is the child able to distinguish between interesting and important ideas? Able to reflect on author intentions?)*

- **Evaluating:** What did you think about this piece? Why do you think the author wrote this? How might you use this information? *(Document the child's ability to evaluate a variety of kinds of text.)*

General Questions

- What are the child's strengths in terms of reading comprehension?
- What evidence is there for growth?
- Which topics and genres does the child prefer?
- In which settings does the child appear to be most comfortable exploring strategies?

Questions for Students

- What strategies do I use to be a successful reader/listener?
- What could I work on?
- Why do I read? How else would I like to use reading? How could I learn to do that?

Figure 3–4 Questions for Documentation

The questions from Figure 3–4 may help you get started with conferencing and talking with small groups. Figure 3–5 provides a self-evaluation form that may help you organize your observations and planning.

A Final Thought

It takes time to become a proficient comprehender. Supporting your students in using and discussing comprehension strategies for authentic purposes is a good way to help them work toward proficiency. If children leave your classroom familiar with terms such as *retell, visualize, predict, monitor, evaluate, question*, and *connect*, and if meaningful experiences have shown them how these strategies enhance their meaning making, they will be well on their way to becoming independent, strategic readers.

As you teach, it is important to avoid awkwardly forcing strategy use just to feel like you've taught something. The idea is to teach strategies when they will give meaning to text or when they will support children's real-life work in the classroom. We don't want children feeling like they must always retell, always make a connection, or always answer postreading questions. Teach strategies when the time is right, and children will embrace them as part of their meaning-making efforts.

Teacher Self-Evaluation and Instructional Planning

	Students have had experiences that specifically encourage exploration of this strategy. *Record dates and experiences.*	The class has struggled with this strategy. *Record dates and specific difficulties.*	Children who need extra support. *Record dates, names, and specific difficulties.*
Predicting and Inferring			
Purpose Setting			
Retelling			
Questioning			
Monitoring			
Visualizing			
Connecting			
Deciding What's Important			
Evaluating			

Figure 3–5

4

WORKING WITH THE STRATEGIES
WHOLE-CLASS, SMALL-GROUP, AND INDIVIDUAL INSTRUCTION

First-Grade Classroom

Jacob has just begun working on an oral presentation about dinosaurs. Sharp pencil in hand and a stack of books before him, he opens one of the books and begins to copy words from the first page. His teacher provides some strategy support.

CHRISTIAN: Jacob, try a picture walk, and write what *you* think.

JACOB: But I want to copy.

Christian and Jacob turn through the pages of the book, talking about the pictures and reading short bits of text until the child generates some ideas that he records using invented spelling.

Dozens of teaching techniques may be used to help children develop reading comprehension strategies. This chapter offers a set of strategy explorations that are particularly appropriate for young children. The chapter is organized into nine sections, one for each of the strategies outlined in Chapter 2. You may implement the explorations in whole-class, small-group, or individualized settings. Observing your students and carefully considering your goals for them will help you to choose the strategy explorations that best meet their needs. As a rule of thumb, try to teach the strategies as they serve authentic purposes. This will help children understand why they should learn them. For example, constructing an informational text organizer may be a useful way to help children decide what's important in a text. But this use *in itself* is probably not as advantageous as using the organizer, say, to collect information for a class book. Similarly, using a story map may be a way to help children learn to focus on key story elements, but this use *in itself* is probably not as advantageous as filling out the map to use as a tool for a dramatic retelling.

To help children engage effectively in the explorations requires modeling, thinking aloud, and scaffolding on your part. As your students begin to use the strategies independently, you should continue to observe them, providing support and further modeling as needed. Collecting work samples and anecdotal notes will help to ensure that your support and modeling are tailored to your students' evolving needs. If you teach kindergarten or first grade, many of your students will not *independently* engage with the explorations this year and many of their explorations will occur through listening rather than reading experiences. But the modeling and support you provide now are important because they help children connect with and learn from text and build a strong foundation for future reading.

Ways to Support Predicting and Inferring

Prediction Discussions

Predicting involves making educated guesses about what might be found in a text. Before and during reading, encourage your students to make predictions about the content and genre of the text, and discuss with them how spending a little time on this activity can tune them in to what they are about to read. The Teacher Talk box shows examples of teaching questions that support these processes.

Teacher Talk: Prediction Discussions

- How does thinking about the cover of a book help you get ready to read?
- Looking at the cover, what do you predict this book might be about?
- Do you think this is fiction or nonfiction? *With fiction, ask:* What do you predict will happen? *With nonfiction, ask:* What do you predict you will learn?
- As you read, are your predictions confirmed?
- What further predictions can you make?
- How does predicting help you as a reader?

Inference Discussions

Inferring involves using personal knowledge and experience to construct meanings that are not explicitly stated in a text. When readers infer, they round out and fill in what the author has written, giving the piece a personal texture and making it whole from their own perspectives. Encourage your students to infer before, during, and after reading. The Teacher Talk box shows some examples.

Teacher Talk: Inference Discussions

- The author didn't tell us how the whale feels about being tangled in this net, but based on what we've read so far, what can you infer?
- These maps show that the square miles of rain forest on our planet have dwindled in the past one hundred years. What can you infer will happen if action is not taken?
- Look at Papa Bear's face. Based on the illustration, what can you infer about how he feels?
- Chrysanthemum used to run to school, but today she's dragging her feet. Based on what we've read, what can you infer are her reasons for taking this action?
- How does taking time to think about inferences help us understand what we read?

Written Predictions and Inferences

When students have some experience with predicting and inferring orally, invite them to write down their predictions and inferences as a way to make them more concrete. A simple prompt can help:

I predict that _____ because _____.

I infer that _____ because _____.

After providing opportunities for students to discuss what they have written, be sure to provide opportunities for them to determine whether their predictions or inferences were confirmed or disconfirmed.

Activating Prior Knowledge

Encourage your students to think about their prior knowledge as they read and listen. Activating prior knowledge is an important component of predicting and inferring because it gets children to think about what they know and feel about a topic. The Teacher Talk box includes a set of general questions that support children's activation of prior knowledge, followed by an example of a teacher modeling how she uses prior knowledge to predict and infer.

Teacher Talk: Activating Prior Knowledge

General Questions

- Think about what you know about this topic.
- Have you seen or experienced something like this before?
- How do your knowledge and ideas help you read and understand the text?

Example:

- Today's newspaper contains another article about that bear cub. To understand it best, it will help me to think about what I know already. From yesterday's article, I remember that she's been going into people's yards. My *prediction* is that the article will say that she's been doing other things—that's why she made the news again.
- The title is *Cub's Curiosity May Cost Her Life*. What could I *infer* from this?

Text Walks

Text walks are another tool for making predictions and inferences. Before reading a text, encourage students to turn through the pages, making predictions and inferences based on the pictures, the narrative, and the text format. Students may also predict key words they think they may find. Picture and text walks give children a general sense of what they are about to read and familiarize them with the language and vocabulary they may encounter (Clay 1985).

Ways to Support Purpose Setting and Purpose Meeting

Using Informational Text Features

In order to engage in efficient reading of informational text, it is necessary for children to learn to set purposes and to use text features to meet those purposes. To facilitate these processes, show your students how readers often approach a reading event with a question or curiosity in mind and then use tables of contents, indexes, headings, and text walks to determine which parts will help them achieve their reading goals. Text features help readers select only the parts that they need in order to meet their reading goals.

Reading for Pleasure

In the world outside of school, literature is often read purely for pleasure, entertainment, or to satisfy a personal curiosity. This makes it important that children in classroom settings have plenty of opportunities to set such purposes. Above all else, we want children to come to know reading as a pleasurable, satisfying act that need not be tied to instruction. To support your students' development of setting and meeting purposes related to pleasure, give them lots of opportunities for independent and partner reading. Permit them to choose their own books, to articulate why they have chosen them, and to reflect on whether their purposes have been met.

Charting Questions and Answers

KWL charts (Ogle 1986), typically used with informational text, are an excellent tool for learning to set purposes and follow through with them (see Figure 4–1). To model the use of a KWL chart, I recommend the following procedures:

1. Before reading, think aloud about the topic and record what you know about it in the What I Know column (the children could help).

2. In the What I Wonder column, list what you (and the children) wonder about or want to know.

3. As you read, focus your attention on answering the questions as well as on gathering other important information that you may not have considered before reading.

4. List what you have learned in the What I Have Learned column.

5. Highlight the questions that have been answered (from the What I Wonder column) and place a check by those that still need answering.

6. Discuss how you will answer the unanswered questions.

7. Discuss how you will use the information from the chart (to write an article, to make a web for sharing, to make a poster).

8. Arrange for groups of children or individuals to construct their own KWL charts. Observe and provide scaffolding as needed.

Gathering Information with a Specific Purpose in Mind

To teach children to gather information with a specific purpose in mind, collect a text set on a topic that relates closely to your social studies or science curriculum. Use one of the texts to show children how you set a purpose, and then read for information that will support your learning about that topic. For example, "I want to know how

KWL Chart

Name: _____

Topic: _____

What I Know:	What I Wonder:	What I Have Learned:

Figure 4–1

echolocation works, so I'm going to read this section and jot down what I find."

Invite your students to engage in the same processes. For example, "At this center, we have ten books about bats. Your job is to use your information sheet (see Figure 4–2) to write or draw all of the things you see bats eating. We'll use the information for our class bat book." Or, "Min's group is studying the endangerment of sea creatures. Today, they are reading to make a list of all of the things that endanger sea creatures. They're going to use the information for the posters they are going to display at the community center."

Gathering specific information helps children build new knowledge about a topic and provides a framework for discussing the information with peers. The information can be used to prepare oral or written reports, to make informative posters, to write fact books, to write informative letters, and overall, to contribute to the content area inquiries in your classroom.

Ways to Support Retelling

Oral Retellings

Invite your students to retell. Oral retelling of fiction or nonfiction is a way to carefully rethink what was read and to bring ideas to a talking place where they can be explored with others. When listening to children retell stories, many teachers expect a logically sequenced *summary* in which reference is made to the characters, the setting, the problem, the resolution, and the theme if one is obvious. (For a distinction between *summary* and *synthesis*, please see Chapter 2.) The wall chart featured in Figure 4–3 offers a simple guide to remind story retellers what to include.

With informational text, teachers typically expect a statement about the topic, a description of the setting if relevant, and an expression of understanding of key concepts. Key concepts may be expressed as a *summary* or a *synthesis*. Figure 4–4 contains a wall chart of possibilities to include in informational text retellings.

You can help children develop these generic forms of retelling by modeling and thinking aloud about how you decide what to include in a retelling and by retelling texts together with them using any of the strategies described in this section.

Story Maps

Make story maps available to your students. Story maps are excellent tools for organizing the retelling of fiction. The story maps shown in Figures 4–5, 4–6, and 4–7 are designed to help children remember to include key elements. Children can write about the elements or draw

Gathering Information from Text

Topic: _____

Question: _____

Findings:

Figure 4–2

Retelling Stories

- Title and Author

- Important Characters

- Setting

- Problem or Goal

- Events

- Resolution

Figure 4–3

52

Retelling Informational Text

- Title and Author

- Topic and Setting

- How Text Is Organized

- Important Ideas, Information, or Events

- Why You Read This

- Why Author Wrote This

Figure 4–4

Story Sequencing Map

Title _____

Beginning

Middle

End

Figure 4–5

General Story Map

Title _____

Characters	Setting
Problem	**Resolution**

Figure 4–6

Detailed Story Map

Title _____

Characters and Setting	Problem

Events (draw lines to make as many boxes as you need)

Resolution	Theme

Figure 4–7

them on the maps. When modeling how to write in key elements, focus on synthesizing, or telling the gist, rather than creating a detailed outline.

Informational Text Organizers

Use informational text organizers to help children organize their thinking about information gleaned from nonfiction. Figures 4–8, 4–9, and 4–10 offer simple maps for retelling and rethinking informational text.

The informational text map (Figure 4–8) provides a space for students to state a purpose and then record three important ideas that connect with that purpose.

The exposition web is a tool that helps students categorically organize information from what they are reading. Figure 4–9 shows the start of an exposition web on dolphins.

The flow map (Figure 4–10) is used to revisit or retell a story or happening (fiction or nonfiction) that is sequenced in some logical way. Only key events are drawn or written in the boxes. In modeling how to develop a flow map, focus on synthesizing events rather than creating a detailed summary. Children may create their own flow map organizers by drawing boxes on a piece of paper and using arrows to connect them or by working with half sheets of paper that are eventually stapled together. Working with half sheets is useful to many children because this allows them to reorganize their ideas once they have put them on paper.

For other organizers to use with informational text, see Figures 4–17 through 4–24. Because a reader's purpose influences how he or she decides what is important, many of these maps include space for children to state a reading purpose.

Visual Retellings

Use visual retellings as a way for children to revisit a piece of text through drawing, painting, coloring, or sculpting. Visual retellings may be used with fiction or nonfiction. Depending on their purpose, children may create visuals of characters, personalities, settings, problem-resolution sequences, or key events. Captions or a narrative may be added to visual retellings and read chorally as a class, by partners, or by teams.

Retelling with Character and Personality Props

Use character and personality puppets or props as a way for children to draw on concrete, visual information as they structure and restructure their thinking about text. Children may make their own props with paper and colored pencils. Laminate the pieces and fasten

Informational Text Map

Name: _____ Date: _____

Title: _____ Pages: _____

Why I read this book: _____

Picture of Three Important Ideas or Events

1.   2.   3.

Description of the Important Ideas or Events

1.

2.

3.

Exposition Web

Goal: **Learn about dolphins**

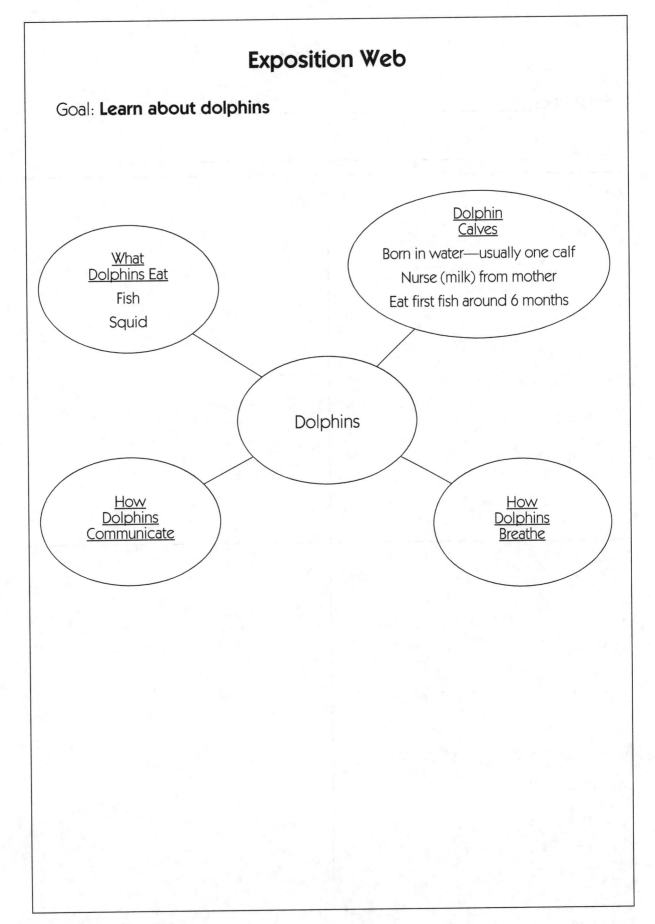

Figure 4–9 Exposition Web

Flow Map

Book Title: _____

Event: _____

1	2
3	4

Figure 4–10

self-stick velcro (for felt boards) or strip magnets (for cookie sheets or magnetic boards) to the back. Or, attach craft sticks to make puppets. As you model the use of props, think aloud about how you decide what the characters or personalities should say. Make the materials available for children during play or center time.

Reenactments

Use reenactments to help children develop insights into the feelings and motivations of characters and personalities and the ways in which they change over time. To introduce reenactment, choose volunteers to stand before the group and act out a scene together. Before they perform, show them how to choose a brief scene and discuss what is important in the scene. For example, with *Cinderella*, you might choose to reenact just the initial encounter between Cinderella and her wicked stepsisters. With *The Princess and the Pea*, you might reenact just the scene in which the princess cannot sleep because she can feel the pea her prospective mother-in-law has hidden under her mattresses and eiderdown beds.

Reenactments typically are brief and occur without a great deal of planning, but if you want to use a whole book, a story web or flow map is useful in guiding the process.

Ways to Support Questioning

Noticing Questions

Life in school is full of questions, and reading events are no exception. Hundreds of questions naturally emerge around reading events, and we want children to know that asking and answering them is a natural and important part of learning. As your students participate in read-alouds, guided reading, partner reading, and individual reading, actively listen for and draw attention to their questions. Questions signify a teachable moment—a time to teach a concept as well as a strategy for finding the answer. If the answer is readily available in the text, model how to find it, or support the child in finding it. If the answer needs to be found elsewhere, write it down, and come back to it later. Point out to children that when they have questions while reading, it is often useful to mark the related area in the text with a sticky note or to write the questions down, so they can return to them and answer them later.

Understanding Question-Answer Relationships

An important part of helping children develop the strategy of questioning involves helping them consider where the answers to their questions might be found. Ask questions such as those found in the

Teacher Talk box (based on Raphael 1986) to help students understand question-answer relationships.

> ### Teacher Talk: Question-Answer Relationships
> - Where could we find the answer?
> - Is the answer in the text?
> - Does the answer require putting together different parts of the text?
> - Does the answer require that we use background knowledge along with information from the text?
> - Do we need the text to answer the question?

Generating Questions and Answers

Because informational text is typically not read from cover to cover, children need to learn to how to locate the particular portions of text that interest them or contain the answers to their particular questions. Generating questions and answers (see Figure 4–11) is a strategy that can help them learn to do so within the framework of your content area inquiries. (KWL charts also can help children develop this strategy.)

As you model this strategy, choose texts that are large enough for all of the children to see. Big books work best. Try to choose genuine questions that you really want answers to. When answers cannot be found in the text, show children how you seek them through other resources. The processes that children learn through generating and answering questions support them in developing content knowledge and becoming independent in their content area inquiries.

Questioning the Author

Use questioning the author (adapted from Beck et al. 1997) as a strategy to support children in delving deeply into text to understand the author's message. As students read, ask questions aimed at helping them to consider the author's goals, intents, and meanings. The Teacher Talk box shows examples of questions for authors.

> ### Teacher Talk: Questioning the Author
> - What is the author trying to tell us?
> - How else could the author say this?
> - Why do you think the author wrote this?
> - What is the author's background?
> - What is his or her point of view on this?

Generating Questions and Answers

1. Choose a book that is related to what you are learning about in science or social studies.

2. Preview the book by looking at the table of contents, headings, and pictures.

3. Decide on something specific you want to find out, and write down at least one question about it.

4. Read what you need to answer the question or to find out more about the topic.

5. Write down what you learn.

6. Rethink or retell what you have learned.

Figure 4–11 Generating Questions and Answers

Ways to Support Monitoring

Stopping to Think

Effective comprehenders regularly monitor their understandings as they read and listen to text. To do so, it helps to stop every so often and rethink what has been read. This ensures that the text has been understood and helps the reader mentally organize the ideas. Modeling how you do this will show children the importance of taking the time to clarify and organize their thinking. To encourage monitoring when individuals, partners, or teams are reading together, ask children to stop every few pages to rethink or retell what they have read so far.

Coding

Provide opportunities for your students to code text. Coding involves readers in marking important ideas, thoughts, and information in the margins of text. For example, children may code **NEW** for "didn't know this before," or **??** for "I don't understand this part." Such activity helps readers purposefully monitor their understandings. You may wish to provide photocopies of text for children to code, or allow your students to use small sticky notes. For young children, very few codes are necessary. Even using one or two is enough to learn the process. Figure 4–12 offers some possibilities.

Repairing Meaning

We have seen that effective readers actively monitor their comprehension as they read. When something doesn't make sense, they recognize it and use fix-up strategies to repair their meaning. Figure 4–13 offers a wall chart of fix-up strategies for children to explore on a daily basis. As you read with children, model how you use these strategies and encourage them to try them out on their own when they are reading independently or with peers.

Making Sense of New Vocabulary

Part of learning to monitor involves developing strategies for determining the meanings of unknown words. Figure 4–14 details seven key vocabulary strategies to model and think about with your students. Figure 4–15 features the strategies on a wall chart to be used for instruction or for children's independent reference.

Ways to Support Visualizing

Visualization Discussions

Visualizing is an important strategy because it prompts readers and listeners to use their personal knowledge and experiences to

Codes for Text

☺ ☺   Discuss this part with partner or group.

? ?   I don't understand this part.

+ +   I can use this part for my project.

NEW   I didn't know this before.

PC   Personal Connection

CBT   Connection Between Texts

Figure 4–12 Codes for Text

Fix-Up Strategies

- Reread

- Read on

- Read aloud

- Read slowly

- Check punctuation

- Look at the illustrations

- Look at special text features

- Figure out any confusing words

- Talk with a friend; retell together

- Ask for help

Figure 4–13 Fix-Up Strategies

Teaching Vocabulary Strategies

- **Predict or infer the meaning.** "What *could* this word mean?" "Let me reread this part to see if my guess would make sense (semantics) and sound right (syntax)."

- **Reread or read on to see if the meaning is clarified.** "If I reread or keep reading, maybe I'll understand this word better."

- **Check the surrounding sentences for a definition.** "Does the author tell me what this means?" "Sometimes definitions are found right in the text. Sometimes they are found in the margins."

- **Look at word parts.** "Does this word have any smaller words or word parts?" "If I notice the word *cycle* in *unicycle*, I have a clue to what it means." "If I notice the *-ing* in *skiing*, it makes the word easier to read."

- **Skip the word.** "Sometimes we don't need to understand the word to get the gist of what we are reading."

- **Use the illustrations.**

- **Try the glossary.**

- **Ask for help.**

Figure 4–14 Teaching Vocabulary Strategies

New Word?

- Predict or infer the meaning.

- Reread or read on to see if the meaning is clarified.

- Check the surrounding sentences for a definition.

- Look at word parts.

- Skip the word.

- Use the illustrations.

- Try the glossary.

- Ask for help.

Figure 4–15

understand text more deeply. Ask questions such as those in the Teacher Talk box to facilitate children's visualization processes.

> ## Teacher Talk: Visualization
>
> - What do you see in your mind as I read this?
> - What might you hear?
> - What might you smell?
> - What might you taste?
> - What might you feel or touch?
> - How does visualization help you understand, enjoy, or appreciate the text?

Drawing

Invite students to listen to or read a piece of poetry, fiction, or nonfiction and then draw what they have seen in their minds (something that is not illustrated in the text or a scene for which you have not shown the illustrations). Tell them what they will be doing beforehand, so they can listen to the text in a way that will help them meet this goal. To get them started, you may wish to prompt with the following:

- Draw a part of the setting.
- Draw a character or personality at a particular point in time.
- Draw an object.
- Draw an event.
- Draw an image evoked by a line of poetry.

When you model, show children how you listen to the author's language. Take the time to think aloud about how things might look, sound, smell, taste, and feel, and try to convey this in your art. As the children work on their own drawings, have the text available for them or read the text aloud to them several times.

Exchanging Drawings

Arrange for children to listen to a poem written by a peer and draw the visual images it conveys. Such activity helps readers and writers tune in to the language of description and explore the ways in which reading and writing may be enhanced by mental images. Before inviting children to engage in this activity, use a child's piece of writing to demonstrate the process.

Story Theatre

Teach your students to dramatize the stories they read. *Story theatre* (Cullinan and Galda 1998) involves the oral reading of poems, folktales, or stories with lots of action and little dialogue. The narrator (a teacher or child) reads aloud while listeners enact the parts. Story theatre encourages children to visualize and physically explore the events and actions of a piece and, therefore, experience it more deeply.

Ways to Support Connecting

Personal Connections

When children personally connect with text, they activate their prior knowledge about all kinds of things—personal experiences, local happenings, world events, characters and personalities—and use it to construct meaning. Ask questions such as those in the Teacher Talk box to support children in making personal connections.

Teacher Talk: Personal Connections

Tell or write about:

- something this text reminded you of
- a connection between something we've read and something you already knew
- a connection between something we've read and something in your own life
- a particular character or personality with whom you identified

---

Story Connections

Invite students to tell personal stories about the experiences they've had with the topic at hand, whether it be from fiction, nonfiction, or poetry. Allow for children's personal stories to be a way of connecting with literature.

Character and Personality Connections

Part of children's connecting with literature involves considering links between their own experiences and those of the characters and personalities about whom they are reading. Considering such links deepens children's understandings of the motives behind character and personality actions and helps them learn to consider multiple views and perspectives. Use Figure 4–16 as an organizer to help children engage in this process.

Character/Personality Connections

Book Title: _____

My Name: _____

Character or Personality Name: _____

Draw or write something about yourself.	Draw or write something about the character or personality you have chosen.

Describe the connection between yourself and the character or personality:

Figure 4–16

Knowledge Connections

Knowledge connections help children become aware of their learning by inviting them to consider links between what they have read and what they already knew about a topic. Use the organizer in Figure 4–17 to help children engage in this process.

Connections Between Texts

Exploring connections between texts helps children piece together and build concepts about the world. Connections may focus on characters, personalities, settings, themes, topics, genres, or two books by the same author. To foster such connections, show students how to use a Three-Column Comparison chart (Figure 4–18), a Venn diagram (Figure 4–19), or a Connections Between Texts organizer (Figure 4–20).

Graffiti Boards

Help students connect with text by arranging for them to listen to a book as they sit in small groups, each with a large piece of paper in the middle (Short, Harste, and Burke 1996). Tell the students that you will occasionally stop reading and invite them to write or draw graffiti that shows a connection they have made. Early on, model and give specific suggestions, such as the following:

- Write about a connection you notice between this book and (name the title of another book).
- Write about something that connects this book with what you already knew.
- Make a picture of something you already knew; add to it something new you have learned.
- Make a picture about something you found interesting.
- Write about something with which you have made a personal connection.

After the reading, allow children to use their graffiti either as a discussion starter or to create a new, unified piece such as a web or chart. The common focus provides a good context for constructing new knowledge together.

Ways to Support Children in Deciding What's Important

Discussions About What Is Important

Books contain many interesting things to pay attention to, but there are times when a reader's specific purpose warrants paying attention to certain ideas or points. Use purpose-oriented small- and whole-

Knowledge Connections

Name: _____

Book Title: _____

Topic: _____

Draw or write something you already knew about the topic:	Draw or write something new you've learned from reading:

Figure 4–17

Three-Column Comparison Chart

Topic: _____

Connection Between: _____

Book One Title:	Book Two Title:	Both Books

Figure 4–18

Venn Diagram

Topic: _____

Connection between _____ and _____

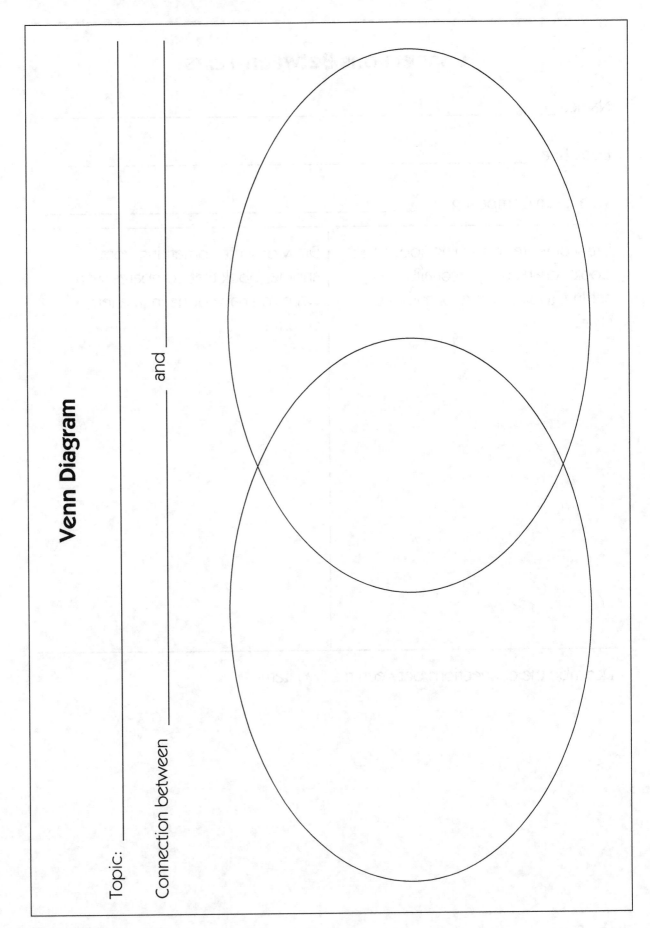

Figure 4–19

Connections Between Texts

Name: _____

Book Title: _____

What I Am Comparing: _____

Draw or write something about one book's character, personality, setting, topic, theme, or author's style.	Draw or write something from another book that compares with what you have done in the left column.

Describe the connections between the two items:

Figure 4–20

group discussions to help students learn to tune in to particular ideas. As you teach, keep in mind that a reader's purpose shapes what he or she determines to be key. For example, an open-ended statement such as "Let's see what we can learn about bread" leads to a different set of ideas about what is important than "Let's see how many different kinds of bread we can find." Either approach is valuable, depending on the reader's goal. Ask questions such as the following found in the Teacher Talk box to support children in learning to make decisions about what is important in text.

Teacher Talk: Deciding What's Important

- What is our purpose?
- Given our purpose, what is important to us in this section?
- What does the author think is important for us to understand here? How do you know?
- What is this section about, mainly?
- How does thinking about our purpose help us decide what's important?

Ideas and Details Chart

There are times when readers and writers need to distinguish between important ideas and interesting details. Children can use ideas and details charts (see Figure 4–21) to help organize their thinking about these two concepts.

Time Lines

Show students how to use time lines to identify and track major happenings in an event or story. Time lines are used primarily with pieces that are sequenced in time order. Figure 4–22 shows a time line based on the book *Black Bear Cub* (Lind 1994).

Sequencing

Sequencing activities help children make discoveries about how authors organize text. Knowing about organization is key to locating ideas in text and to discovering what the author thinks is important. To work with sequencing, photocopy a piece of text that relates in some way to your curriculum. Cut it into three or four parts. Laminate the parts and invite students to put them back together in order. Try recipes, short stories, paragraphs from longer stories, notes, and sections from nonfiction books. Be sure to draw your students' attention to the text structure and to any language the author uses to set up that structure (*first, next, most important*).

Ideas and Details Chart

Topic: _____

Book: _____

Purpose for Reading: _____

Important Ideas: Record ideas that are important to meeting your goals for reading this text.	**Interesting Details:** Record interesting details that are connected to the important ideas.

Figure 4–21

Goal for Reading: Learn about life cycle of bears

Key Events	–black bear cubs born –stay in den for a few days	–cubs climb and play –mother forages	–cubs playful –learn about dangers –learn to find food, water	–family finds another den	–family sleeps
Time	early spring	first leaves on trees	summer	autumn	winter

Figure 4–22 Time Line

Research Charts

Use research charts as tools for collecting and comparing important information from different sources. Figure 4–23 shows the start of a research chart on pigs. The headings on the chart help students decide what is important as they read. Such charts are useful when different groups are studying different items that fall within the same semantic category; for example, *cows*, *pigs*, *chickens*, and *sheep* all fall within the semantic category of *farm animals*. If each group is studying one farm animal, when you compile the results, you have a new and more complete picture of the category.

Feature Analysis Charts

As with research charts, feature analysis charts help children read or listen just for the information they need on a topic. Feature analysis is useful when children would benefit from comparing a number of items that fall within a semantic category (such as *fish*, *vehicles*, *vegetables*, *planets*, or *trees*). Figure 4–24 shows the start of a feature analysis chart on trees. Feature analysis may be taught in the following way:

1. Develop a chart that is appropriate to your topic or allow your students to help you develop the chart. When students eventually develop their own charts, they are likely to need lots of support in determining the categories for analysis, especially at first.

2. Model for children how you are able to fill in some of the chart based on what you know already.

Research Chart
Topic: PIGS

Information from Books	What do they look like?	What do they eat?	What shelter do they need?	What care do they need?	What are their uses?
Title:					
Title:					
Title:					

Figure 4–23 Research Chart

3. Model how you read one or more pieces of text to fill in the rest of the chart. Use this opportunity to show students how you use text features such as the glossary, table of contents, and headings to locate specific information rather than reading information that is unnecessary for meeting your reading goals.

4. When the chart is complete, show students different ways that the collected information may be interpreted and used. For example, reading down the Uses column for trees will give a quick synopsis of all the ways trees are used.

Genre Studies

In a typical genre study, children read a genre-based text set, engage in response activities, compose their own pieces in that genre, and engage in numerous discussions about the nature of the genre. In terms of comprehension, genre studies are important because they

Feature Analysis Chart
Topic: Trees

Trees	Lobed?	Serrated, Toothed, or Smooth?	Simple or Compound?	Uses	Other Information
Apple	no				
Cherry					
Cottonwood		finely toothed	simple		
Maple					
Red Oak	yes			furniture, acorns	
Walnut			compound		
White Oak		smooth			

Figure 4–24 Feature Analysis Chart

help children develop familiarity with the content and structures of various categories of literature. This familiarity helps them locate and identify important ideas as they read. For example, children who are familiar with recipe books have expectations about the kind of information these books will contain and about how the information will be organized. Such expectations form a mental outline that supports their identification and organization of important information and makes their construction of meaning efficient.

To organize a genre study, collect a text set (three to twenty books) that will connect with your curricular goals. The books may be read in whole- or small-group settings and should also be made available for individual reading and browsing. As you read the books with children, and engage with them in response activities, help them do the following:

- connect with and learn from the individual books in the set
- make connections between books
- learn about the generic features of the text set
- compose their own pieces in that genre

Following are some ideas for getting started.

Alphabet books

Help children notice and describe the many topics and features of alphabet books. After studying various texts, help children choose themes for writing their own books. Talk about the number of pages the books will have and why, and decide on the kinds of illustrations to include. Less experienced children may wish to write only the letters of the alphabet to go with the illustrations, while older children may write words or sentences.

Autobiographies

After reading a few autobiographies with your students, and engaging in response activities that help them explore their content and format, invite children to write their own. To do so, invite them to write about or draw key early memories, important stories they have heard about their early lives, and special life events. Children can use time lines or flow charts to plan, or they can write one event per page and then organize the pages in some meaningful sequence.

Biographies

A good biography tells the story of another person's life and helps the reader understand the historical context in which that life was lived. Emphasize these characteristics as you share biographies with your students, and help them see that biographies are made up of a series of important ministories. To help students construct biographies of their own, discuss possible people to write about. It might be easiest to write about classmates or family members—people with whom they feel comfortable. Children can get their information by interviewing both their subjects and the subjects' acquaintances. To remember what they hear, they can audiotape, take notes, or draw pictures. They can use time lines for planning or write one event per page and then organize their pages in some meaningful order. (Biographies are not always presented in time order. For example, they may begin in the present, or they may include flashbacks.)

Number books

Share a number book text set, discussing text features and content. Invite your students to create books of their own, appropriating the style (or combination of styles) of the authors they are reading.

Storybooks

Engage children in a genre study of fantasy books, fairy tales, tall tales, or fables. Bring in several books to read and browse; discuss their distinguishing characteristics and write a storybook as a class or allow children to write their own. Possible planning devices include time lines and story webs.

Recipe books

Bring in a set of recipe books for browsing. As a group, discuss their content (you'll find more than just recipes!) and text features. Help children write recipes for a class book.

Ways to Support Evaluating

Evaluation Discussions and Written Responses

Evaluating involves all kinds of thinking, including

- critiquing and establishing opinions
- considering author intents and viewpoints
- analyzing uses of language
- preparing to use and apply new information gained from reading

Use the questions in Figure 4–25 to stimulate evaluative thinking either through oral discussions or writing.

Advertisements

An important part of evaluation is establishing tastes, preferences, and opinions. To provide opportunities for children to do so, model how to create a brochure, poster, magazine advertisement, or television commercial to publicize a favorite book. Think aloud about

- what you liked about the narrative and illustrations
- how the book could be used
- who you think would like the book
- any interesting uses of language
- any interesting ways of dealing with characters and personalities

Ask students questions such as those in Figure 4–25 to stimulate their thinking. Then regularly provide them with time to create their own advertisements, allowing time for sharing.

Book reviews

Book reviews are another forum for learning to evaluate text. The following procedures may be used to teach children to review books:

Talking About Text

- What do you think about this piece? Why?

- What do you think of the illustrations? Why?

- Why do you think the author wrote this?

- Who should read this? Why?

- What do we know about the author? How do you think the author's background shapes what he or she writes?

- Do you agree with the author's views?

- Are different groups of people portrayed fairly?

- Fiction: Do the characters seem real? Could this really happen?

- Nonfiction: Is this easy to understand? What do you think of the examples?

- What do you think of the way the author uses language (imagery, alliteration, rhyme)?

- How can you use this information?

Figure 4–25 Talking About Text

1. Read several books and their reviews with children.
2. Model writing your own review.
3. Write a review together as a class.
4. Give children time to browse the class library for books they have liked—or not liked.
5. Assign children to write their own reviews.

Individual reviews may be included in a class newsletter or magazine, or a compiled set can be bound together and placed in the class library.

Polls

Inviting children to conduct opinion polls is another way to promote evaluation. Children may conduct polls about preferred books, genres, authors, illustrators, topics, or response activities. To get started, use Figure 4–26 to equip teams with a list of names of the children in the class. Teams write evaluation questions and possible answer options on the form. For example, "Which author do you prefer? Leo Lionni or Eric Carle? Why?" "Which type of response do you prefer? Drawing, writing, or talking? Why?" Pollsters place a check under each interviewee's choice and document a qualitative response in the Why? column. Children tally all responses and report the results to the class.

Book talks

Book talks provide another forum for learning to evaluate. The following procedures may be used to teach children how to give book talks.

1. Use the form featured in Figure 4–27 to plan and model a book talk. Be sure to use an opening line that will draw in your audience; then tell what you liked about the book; and finally, sum up with a line that will further entice potential readers.

2. Read a second book with your students and show them how to fill out the form. Solicit their help in deciding what to write down.

3. Invite two or three child volunteers to use the form created in step 2 to model a practice book talk for the class.

4. Arrange for individuals or small groups to give book talks. If you have a large planning calendar in your room, encourage students to sign up to give their book talks as part of your regular morning meeting or read-aloud session.

Opinion Poll

Names Place children's names in the spaces below.	Which do you prefer? Write choices in the spaces below. Place checks in the boxes.			Why? Ask pollsters why they prefer their choice, and record the responses in the space below.
	Choice 1:	Choice 2:	Choice 3:	

Figure 4–26

Book Talk Planning Form

Name: _____

Date of Book Talk: _____

Title of Book: _____

Opening Line: _____

_____

_____

What You Liked About the Book: _____

_____

_____

_____

_____

Closing Line: _____

_____

_____

Figure 4–27

Evaluation Forms

Book evaluation forms are a simple, fun way to share opinions about books. Encourage students to fill out the forms (see Figures 4–28 and 4–29) and place them in the class library. The child writes the book title and author on one side of the form and places a check on the appropriate blanks on the other side. File the cards in alphabetical order so that others can easily use the reviews as they select books to read.

Good Fiction?

_____ Do the characters seem real?

_____ Is this a good story?

_____ Does the author make you want to see what happens at the end?

_____ Are the illustrations interesting?

_____ Do the illustrations add to the meaning of the author's words?

Figure 4–28

Good Nonfiction?

_____ Is it easy to find information?

_____ Is the book interesting to children?

_____ Is the book easy to understand?

_____ Does the author make you care about the topic?

_____ Are the table of contents, headings, index, glossary, and illustrations helpful?

Figure 4–29

5

Organizing and Implementing Literature Circles

First-Grade Classroom

Yesterday, Christian read aloud *On the Way to Christmas* (Shpakow 1991) to her first-grade students. In preparation for literature circles, the children have written down their ideas about what the author could have done differently. Amelia uses her written piece as a starting place for her group's conversation:

AMELIA: [*referring to her written ideas*] I think the little girl could say [*to the teddy bear*], "You are so pretty and I love you so much that you are so new and I want to keep you forever."

CAYLA: The teddy bear was *old*. How come you said it was new?

AMELIA: I wanted to say that because I thought it could be new to her.

CAYLA: But, it smelled.

AMELIA: Yeah, but I made a different ending . . .

In early childhood classrooms, literature circles typically involve children in reading or listening to a book, responding individually, and then discussing their thoughts in small groups. Very young children may take one or two days to complete the process; older children may take up to two or three weeks.

As the vignette shows, literature circles promote thoughtful exploration of *book content*. The individual response time has given

Amelia and Cayla a chance to organize and think through their ideas about the book. The peer discussion provides them with opportunities to articulate their ideas, get feedback on them, and see how others have interpreted and responded to the book. When children are given space to let their ideas roam together, new paths of thinking are explored, and new interpretations of text are constructed.

Thoughtful exploration of *comprehension strategies* occurs through literature circles as well. In the example, Amelia and Cayla are *evaluating*; they are learning to consider the choices that authors make and how they influence the outcomes of a story. To prepare the class for this experience, Christian modeled her own evaluative thinking about the text and used metacognitive language so that the children would understand what she was doing.

Throughout this chapter we will explore ways to organize and implement literature circles with attention to thoughtful exploration of both content and strategies. Figure 5–1 is a good place to begin. It provides an overview of the phases of a literature circle.

Establishing the Environment

To gain insight into the intricacies of organizing literature circles, we will take a look at the way Christian Bush gets them started in her first-grade classroom. For her, the first month of the school year involves helping her students build and adjust to the literacy practices in their new classroom and working toward a community that is characterized by warm literacy relationships. It comes down to this: if literature circles are going to be a success, the children must know the *discourses* associated with publicly sharing writings, drawings, and ideas, and they must feel *safe* in taking the risks that are necessary to do so.

Teaching the Discourses

To help her students understand the procedures, or *discourses*, associated with literature circles, Christian begins the school year by regularly inviting the class to listen to books, respond by writing or drawing, and share their responses with the whole group. Christian models the procedure by writing and sharing her own responses. Sometimes the possibilities for response are open-ended. For example, children may record (through drawing or writing) what they have learned from a text, a personal connection, or something they found interesting. At other times, Christian asks the children to focus on a particular idea: how they feel about a character's actions, what they would have done in a similar situation, or the problem-resolution sequence. Christian's goal during the first month of school is to help

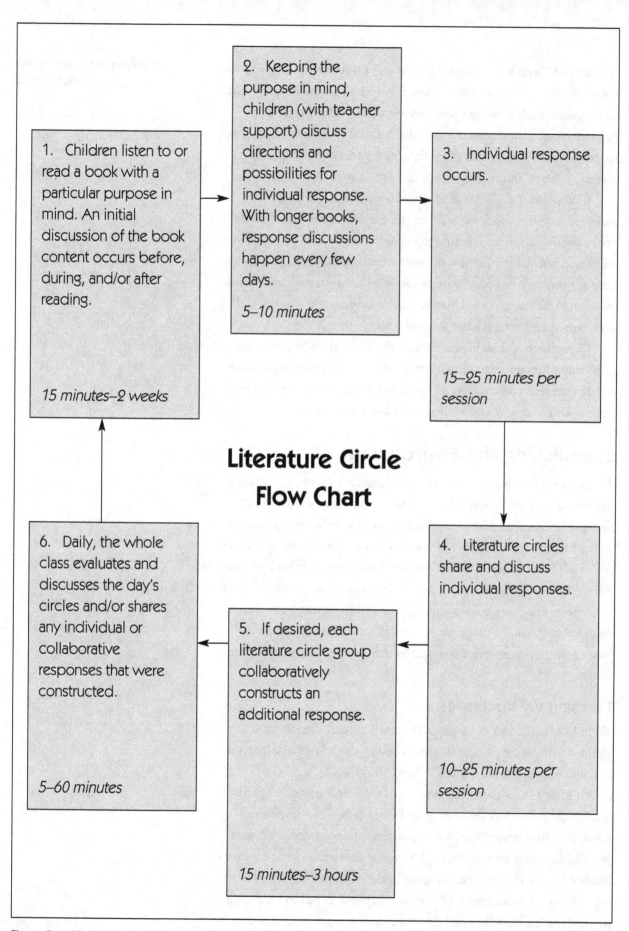

1. Children listen to or read a book with a particular purpose in mind. An initial discussion of the book content occurs before, during, and/or after reading.

15 minutes–2 weeks

2. Keeping the purpose in mind, children (with teacher support) discuss directions and possibilities for individual response. With longer books, response discussions happen every few days.

5–10 minutes

3. Individual response occurs.

15–25 minutes per session

Literature Circle Flow Chart

4. Literature circles share and discuss individual responses.

10–25 minutes per session

5. If desired, each literature circle group collaboratively constructs an additional response.

15 minutes–3 hours

6. Daily, the whole class evaluates and discusses the day's circles and/or shares any individual or collaborative responses that were constructed.

5–60 minutes

Figure 5–1 Literature Circle Flow Chart

her students learn the discourses for listening to, responding to, and sharing ideas about literature.

When her students are familiar with these discourses, Christian invites a small group to demonstrate the literature circle process. First, she reads a book to the whole class and gives the whole class time to respond individually. Then, the small group sits within the larger group, and Christian helps the group members share their responses. Her intention is for the children to use the structures demonstrated early in the year as a scaffold to guide future conversations. She wants the children to remember that each child must share *and* actively listen and that a conversation may ensue around any child's response. Once the students have seen one or two circles modeled in this way, they are ready to set out on their own.

Creating a Sense of Safety

Along with this early instruction in discourses, Christian helps her students feel *safe* by fostering a classroom culture in which children see themselves as being competent to write and talk about literature. From the first day of school, she responds to children who claim they can't write or can't draw with, "Well, show me what you *can* do, so I can help you grow." As these hesitant children get their ideas on paper, Christian helps them understand that literacy develops over time; children do not write or draw like adults, nor does she expect them to do so. For the children who say the book didn't give them any ideas for writing or discussion, Christian helps them find a connection. She asks, "What does this (book, page, picture) make you think about?" "Have you seen or heard something like this before?" For the children who write or say something that is treated as out of whack by the other children, Christian responds with, "Wait. Everyone sees things differently. Let's listen so we can see in a new way." Christian's focus is on developing a classroom culture in which learners will take risks with writing and drawing and will actively and sensitively listen to what others have to say.

Observing, Documenting, and Scaffolding

As the children move into their early literature circles, *observation* is another important component of Christian's instruction. Careful observation is essential for tailoring instruction to meet the children's specific needs. Without well-tailored instruction, children are not likely to automatically fall into deep and thoughtful discussions. The following example illustrates:

> Carlton shares his response to the book his group has
> just read.

MILTON: Interesting

ZEKE: Awesome.

ARCHIE: Pretty amazing.

Roxanne shares her response.

CARLTON: Awesome.

MILTON: Cool.

CAYLA: Good.

The example shows that while the potential for collaborative construction of knowledge is significant, it doesn't always happen, especially during early literature circles. Often, children do not achieve a level of shared understanding or interest upon which to build a conversation. Merely sitting in a circle to share responses or to discuss a book does not guarantee that rich interactions will occur.

To help her students experience the full value of literature circles, Christian spends the year collecting anecdotal notes and writing samples. Her schedule for the first few months involves visiting one or two circles each meeting day. (She typically has five circles running simultaneously.) Through her observations, she systematically discovers who moves easily into literature circles, who is an expert strategy user, who stimulates rich conversations, and who has a tendency to stir up bedlam. She uses these observations to strategically place children in groups and to determine the direction of class discussions about literature circle discourses.

Anecdotal notes serve as an ideal tool for untangling the complexities in classroom interactions and identifying areas that need work. For example, Christian's literature circle notes revealed that many groups were falling into the share-evaluate-share pattern of discourse illustrated in the previous vignette: each time one child shared, the others mostly evaluated but said nothing more. Although on the surface the groups appeared to be operating smoothly, the notes showed that the conversations were rather trifling.

Through her observations, Christian was able to tailor her instruction to meet her groups' specific needs. In an attempt to get them to abandon the share-evaluate-share pattern of discourse, she added a collaborative component to the circles. She began to require that, after sharing and discussing individual responses, each group construct a collaborative response to the literature. The change in process worked well and the children began to engage in more substantive discourses about texts.

Christian also uses the information she collects during literature circles to inform her scaffolding of individual children. For example, when she observed that Jerome was saying very little during literature circles, she began a series of over-the-shoulder conferences with him. As they talked, Christian learned that Jerome was uncomfortable because he could not read what he had written. (Most of the other first graders couldn't read *their* writing either, but Jerome seemed more bothered by this than the others.) Through several conferences, Christian helped Jerome make his text more readable by supporting him with letter formation and spelling and by encouraging him to reread what he had written several times before meeting with the group. She also encouraged him to *tell about* rather than *read* what he had written. With well-tailored scaffolding, Jerome was able to participate more effectively.

As you can see, Christian's procedures for getting literature circles started are aimed at helping children feel safe and helping them learn how to reflect, share, and listen. Early on, she familiarizes students with the general discourses for a literature circle and documents events in ways that enable her to scaffold children toward effective participation. As the children gain experience and independence, she is able to change her support from a focus on discourses and group processes to a more substantive focus on comprehension strategies and book content.

Likewise, as you prepare for literature circles, some important early goals will be to work toward a safe literacy environment in which your students can become confident with sharing their ideas and familiar with basic literature circle routines. Later, you will find more time to focus on strategies and content. As you take notes, focus on children's strengths as well as on the skills and strategies that you want to improve. Figures 5–2 and 5–3 offer some possibilities for organizing your anecdotal note taking.

Getting Your Literature Circles Up and Running

Choosing the Literature

When you feel like your students are ready to try out literature circles, take some time to look for books that will open doors to thoughtful conversation. Thoughtful discussions emerge when children encounter characters and situations they relate to as well as unexpected or unusual twists. As you look for books, ask yourself which might raise interesting questions and provoke intrigue in the eyes of your students. Which books connect with their interests and prior knowledge? Which connect with your curriculum? Which will they want to talk about? Carefully thinking through such questions will

Observation Form for Literature Circles

	I have observed individual students during this phase. *Record dates, names, and student strengths.*	Children who need extra support. *Record dates, names, and specific difficulties.*
Reading or Listening Time		
Individual Response Time		
Group Meeting/ Collaborative Response Time		

Figure 5–2

Observing Individual Students During Literature Circles

Place each student's name in a box. Record dates and observations.

Figure 5–3

help ensure that your students are able to build rich conversations around books.

Reading the Books

Before children read or listen, it is helpful for them to establish a purpose (such as preparing to tell whether they liked the text and why). If you want them to focus on a mutual goal, they (or you) should set it before reading. This will help them concentrate on specific ideas. In early circles especially, a mutual purpose can help get conversations going. After you have set a purpose, you have several options for how the class will read the literature circle texts (see Figure 5–4 for ideas). Given your students' age and experience, decide which would work best for their first literature circles.

Responding Individually

After children have read a book, they independently construct a visual or written response to share with the circle. If long or complex pieces are being used, you may wish to arrange for the children to respond and meet a few times during the reading of the book. Figure 5–5 offers some possibilities for response that are connected to each comprehension strategy described in Chapter 2. It is a good idea to start with teacher-chosen responses. Providing some initial direction on how to respond helps children understand the repertoire of choices available to them. To work toward child-chosen responses, start a wall chart of response ideas with your children.

Supporting the Circles

When the individually constructed responses are complete, students bring them to circles for sharing and discussion. To help groups run smoothly, you may wish to designate a group leader or let children choose a leader for the day. Keeping a record sheet (Figure 5–6) ensures that all children have experiences as leader. Group leaders may be responsible for

- collecting any necessary materials
- beginning the conversation by sharing their ideas first
- ensuring that all voices are heard
- recording information to bring back to the class
- reporting back to the class

Early on, you may find that some groups finish in five minutes or fewer but do not have the kind of in-depth conversations for which you were hoping. Have a plan in place to encourage further reflection. Suggesting a collaborative response (see following section) can help.

Grouping, Texts, and Reading: Flexible Formats

One Book/Whole Class

- Select one book that the whole class would enjoy.

- Read the book aloud to the class. This works especially well with children who are not yet reading print independently. Even with older children, it is a good idea to use this format early on, so that you can familiarize them with literature circle discourses.

Five Books/Small Groups, Partners, or Individuals

- Collect five different books (or six copies each of five different books).

- Introduce each book to the whole class.

- Lay out the books and invite children to place a nametag on their first choice. When six tags have accumulated on a book, that choice is closed.

- Older children may read the books independently, in pairs, or as a group. Parents, grandparents, and/or older students may help read the books to younger children.

Wordless Picture Books/Small Groups, Partners, or Individuals

- Collect a set of wordless picture books (one per child or one per group).

- If you have collected one book per child, arrange for children to explore the books independently before sharing with the group.

- If you have collected one book per group, literature circle members designate a reader or walk through the pages together, telling the story. The children then construct individual responses in preparation for sharing.

Text Set/Small Groups, Partners, or Individuals

- Collect five text sets (seven to ten different books focusing on a common topic, theme, author, or illustrator).

- Introduce each set to the whole class.

- Display the five sets and invite children to place a nametag on their top choice. When six tags have accumulated on a set, that choice is closed.

- Each child chooses from the set a book to read or browse independently, with a peer, or with the group. Children may read a few of the books aloud together.

Figure 5–4 Grouping, Texts, and Reading: Flexible Formats

Responding Collaboratively

After the children have discussed their individual responses with their groups, each group may construct a collaborative response, possibly to share with the whole class. For example, if individuals have focused on documenting interesting words, then the group might decide together on three words to share with the whole class. To foster student independence, as with individual responses, start a collaborative response possibility chart on the wall. Figure 5–7 offers some possibilities. This will enable students to eventually choose the response forms they find most suitable for meeting their purposes. Collaborative responses may be constructed every time literature circles meet or only every so often.

After creating collaborative responses, children need time to share their work with you or the class. Sometimes, sharing with the class is not relevant because the other students do not have enough background on the book or topic to understand the group's response to it. In these cases, a brief sharing with you should suffice.

Encouraging Self-Evaluation

Self-evaluation is an important component of literature circles because it helps children tune in to their roles as learners and become aware of what they are learning. A simple set of prompts (Figure 5–8) can help guide children's self-evaluation. These prompts may be reflected upon orally or in writing.

Providing Time to Grow

Literature circles provide a dynamic medium for children to connect with and learn from books. During the first weeks of literature circles, you will inevitably have lots of adaptations to make and lots of problem solving to do, but don't give up. Just grant your students and yourself a little time to bloom. Nurture them with good books, specific observations about what they are doing well, and suggestions for improving what is not going well. Nurture yourself by listening to students' ideas, talking with colleagues about what you are doing, and allowing yourself to be a learner. With a little time, and with an effort that you are likely to find intellectually stimulating, your students' language and literacy will flower and reseed along paths that continue to surprise and delight you.

Individual Response Possibilities	
Strategy	Using writing or drawing, prepare to discuss the following with your literature circle.
Predicting and Inferring	• one prediction made before or during reading and whether it was confirmed • one inference made before, during, or after reading and whether it was confirmed • an inference about what a character/personality might state to be most important in his or her life/world • an inference about what a character/personality might think about _____ (a school-based, local, national, or international issue)
Purpose Setting	• your goals/purposes/hopes for reading this text and whether they were met or not met • what you noticed during your text walk and how it helped you get ready to read • the information on your KWL Chart (see Figure 4–1) • the information on your Gathering Information from Text sheet (see Figure 4–2)
Retelling	• a synthesis • a summary • the problem-resolution sequence • a story map (see Figures 4–5 to 4–7) • an informational text organizer (see Figures 4–8, 4–9, 4-10, 4–21, and 4–22) • a map that can be used to describe the changing settings • changes in a character or personality
Questioning	• a question • a wondering • a Generating Questions and Answers sheet (see Figure 4–11) • a question for the author
Monitoring	• one thing you learned • a synthesis or summary of part of the text • a section of coded text (see Figure 4–12 for codes) • something that confused you • a record of interesting or new words • a record of important words
Visualizing	• your image of a character or personality • your image of a character or personality at a particular point in time • your image of a part of the setting • your image of an event *(continues)*

Figure 5–5 Individual Response Possibilities

Individual Response Possibilities

Strategy	Using writing or drawing, prepare to discuss the following with your literature circle.
Visualizing (*continued*)	• a picture from the text (marked with a sticky note) with a written reflection of what you might hear, smell, feel, and taste in that scene • your image of a section of text that is not pictured
Connecting	• a personal connection • a feeling you had while reading • something that surprised you • something that interested you • a connection between texts (see Figures 4–18, 4–19, and 4–20) • something you are thinking or feeling now that you've read the text • something this text reminded you of • a character or personality with whom you particularly identified (see Figure 4–16) • a connection between something you've read and something you already knew (see Figure 4–17)
Deciding What Is Important	• a main idea • sticky notes showing key ideas • a diagram, picture, or model that shows what you have learned • an important quote or picture (tell why it's important) • the results of your Ideas and Details chart (see Figure 4–21) • a time line (see Figure 4–22) • sticky notes showing interesting ways the author has organized the text
Evaluating	• an interesting event (tell why it's interesting) • an interesting illustration (tell why it's interesting) • a favorite part or a part you didn't like (tell why) • a favorite character or a character you didn't like (tell why) • what the main character/personality did at a certain point; what you would do in a similar situation (tell why) • an alternative to the resolution • what you think about the illustrations (tell why) • one way you will use information from the text • why you think the author wrote this text • who you think should read this text (tell why) • how you feel about the author's use of language (tell why) • an advertisement or book review (see Chapter 4) • an evaluation form (see Figures 4–28 and 4–29)

Figure 5–5 (*Continued*)

Literature Circle Leaders

Children's Names	Dates as Literature Circle Leader			

Figure 5–6

Collaborative Response Possibilities

Something Interesting

Each group prepares to share something interesting the members observed or discussed about one of the following:

- a topic
- a character
- a setting
- an event
- a theme
- vocabulary
- what the group determined to be most important
- a problem-resolution sequence
- their predictions or inferences
- the illustrations
- the way they visualized
- something new they learned
- how the group felt about the piece
- why the group thinks the author wrote this piece

Collaborative Projects

For collaborative projects, groups may

- write a book review
- create a set of puppets to perform a retelling
- develop a web, map, or time line, or an informational text organizer, for retelling
- create a piece of art (mural, painting, drawing, sculpture) to visually represent some part of the text
- compose a skit based on a scene or event from the book
- compose a script for a readers theatre performance
- gather and display objects representing some element of the text
- build a block structure to represent some part of the text or to represent something the group has learned
- sculpt a scene from a book
- create a labeled diagram to explain some concept from the book
- draw a picture that synthesizes or summarizes part of the book
- develop a book talk (see Figure 4–27)

Figure 5–7

Literature Circle Self-Evaluation

Tell one important thing you learned today.

Tell one important question you asked or comment you made.

Tell what you did to be a good listener.

Tell what you could do to make your group run more smoothly.

Figure 5–8

6

ORGANIZING AND IMPLEMENTING PARTNER READING

First-Grade Classroom

Reclining in a beanbag chair with feet propped on a large pillow, Milton and Tina are taking a picture walk through *Coco Can't Wait* (Gomi 1984):

> MILTON: That house is really far away. They're just giving a close-up . . .

After the picture walk, Milton begins to read the book aloud. Occasionally, Tina helps him monitor, but usually, he self-monitors:

> MILTON: [*reading the text*] "Who no! Grandma is not here." Wait, that's not *who*. *Who* no? That can't be right.

Partner reading in early childhood classrooms typically involves two children in reading a book together and responding to its content through talk or writing. Very young children may take ten to fifteen minutes to complete the process; older children may take up to thirty minutes. Many teachers implement partner reading once or twice a week; some implement it almost every day. Once the procedures are clear to students, many teachers use this time of day, or part of it, to work with guided reading groups.

As the vignette shows, partner reading promotes thoughtful exploration of *book content*. When Milton and Tina read together, they are the authorities. Following their own lines of interest, they pause often to discuss what is happening, spontaneously ask each other questions, and point out interesting illustrations and uses of language. Partner reading also promotes children's exploration of *comprehension strategies*. The vignette shows that before reading, Milton and Tina previewed the text—a good way to familiarize themselves with its content and structure. Then, during the reading, they monitored their understandings and used fix-up strategies as necessary. In early childhood classrooms, partner reading provides a forum for children to explore literature in a nonthreatening context and to learn from one another.

Establishing the Environment

Social Matters

A safe classroom environment is essential to the success of partner reading. When students feel safe in taking the risks involved with exposing their knowledge to other students, they are most likely to try out their tentative ideas and strategies and to readily consider feedback from peers. Children do not learn without experimentation. If they are to become expert at predicting, inferring, setting purposes, retelling, questioning, monitoring, and the like, they must have safe opportunities to explore these strategies.

To promote a sense of safety, it is necessary to work toward a classroom culture in which students recognize that it is permissible to be a learner, one who develops over time. As you and your students discuss discourses for working with partners, help them understand that children develop different strengths at different rates. Some children are already good at playing catch; some are already good at making friends; some are already good at sitting attentively in a group; some are already good at reading. All children have strengths in some areas and all are still developing strengths in others.

Talk explicitly with your students about specific ways they can support one another as readers. Children who are consciously aware of support strategies are more likely to provide effective assistance than children who take over when a partner gets stuck. To get such discussions started, ask your students to brainstorm some ideas about ways to provide support. The Teacher Talk box offers some conversation starters for discussing decoding and comprehension strategies, but it will be most helpful to develop your own questions based on what you observe your students doing. As you discuss the strategies with students, start a wall chart that could be used as a reference when partners are reading together.

> ## Teacher Talk: Strategy Conversations
>
> - When a partner gets stuck on a word, what could you do to help?
> - Does every word that is read incorrectly need to be corrected? For example, if your partner reads *grandma* for *grandmother* or *cat* for *kitty*, does the story need to be interrupted?
> - What could you do when your partner doesn't understand what he or she is reading?
> - What could you do when your partner isn't sure how to respond to the literature?

You may find it helpful to teach the whole class a word-solving strategy to use during partner reading. Figure 6–1 outlines one such strategy. As you teach the strategy, point out that partners benefit more from having time to think than from an overzealous partner who tells all unknown words. However, let them know that it is okay for partners to supply words when readers are unable to solve them. As you observe partners reading together, watch for opportunities to support this strategy.

The Physical Environment

The physical environment in a classroom also contributes to the success of partner reading. Before implementing your program, take stock of the *comfortable* locations in your classroom. Where can children easily sit side by side? Do you have large pillows? Could they be placed against a wall so that children could lean back? Could two sets of partners sit on a couch? Do you have a large rug? Could you pull out a few mats just for partner reading? Could they be placed under a table? In a corner? Behind your desk or a cabinet? Would some children feel more comfortable at a desk or a table? Providing a comfortable environment will help students settle quietly and comfortably into reading.

Peacefulness is another aspect of the environment to consider. Many children find it distracting to read when they are in a noisy or active environment. As you establish the environment for partner reading, be sure to aim for as many secluded areas as possible. More importantly, teach your students to read and talk quietly. When you are discussing with children what is expected of them during partner reading, emphasize the importance of using soft voices. It can be informative to invite two or three sets of partners to demonstrate. First give them a book to read loudly (this is especially illustrative if you

Solving Words

1. Put your finger under the word and think about what would make sense.

2. Try to pronounce the word by thinking about the sounds or word parts.

3. Reread the sentence to see if your pronunciation makes sense.

4. If your pronunciation doesn't work, try again.

5. If you are still stuck, read on to see if the word is clarified later.

Figure 6-1 Solving Words

choose a few of the hams in the class), and then ask them to read softly. Invite the students to discuss the differences in the two conditions and in their respective ability to enjoy the literature and concentrate on making meaning.

When your students are ready to partner read, point out the locations you have established. It may be helpful to create a set of number cards labeled one through fourteen (if you have twenty-eight students) and set them around the classroom in the comfortable locations. Assign each set of partners to a number and ask them to read in that location. Or ask them to choose their location and to continue to use it as long as they remain partners. Partner reading can be an enjoyable learning and bonding time for you and your students. Making an effort to carefully build the social and physical environment will contribute greatly to this potential.

Choosing the Literature

Well-chosen literature is another key to the success of partner reading. Regularly allowing children to choose their own books ensures that partners will be interested in the material and motivated to read it. Many options are available for facilitating student choice:

- Arrange for your students to use their school library visits to choose books for partner reading.

- Gather fourteen sets of books (if you have twenty-eight students) and display them for a day or two. Encourage your students to browse the choices, and when the time comes to read, draw names for partners to make their decisions.

- Allow students to choose books from the class library.

- Encourage students to bring in books from home to share during partner reading.

On occasion, you may wish to assign the literature to be read. For example, you may want children to reread a book they have read in a guided reading group or as part of whole-class instruction. Or you may wish to assign books based on what you have learned about your students' interests.

Along with being interested in the material, we want children to feel successful with their partner reading endeavors. Encouraging them to work with text that they can decode and understand with relative ease will help them become confident as readers. It will also help them develop fluency and fine-tune their independent use of comprehension strategies. However, every partner reading event need not occur with literature that is at the children's independent or instructural level. Allowing children to work with text that they find demanding will challenge them to develop new reading strategies. With a partner in place and a strong desire to make sense of the material, children are often able to read books that may initially appear to be too difficult. As you observe, take note of the materials your students are choosing, and intervene with those who regularly choose material that is either too easy or too difficult.

Teaming the Children

Strategically teaming children for partner reading is another way to foster the success of the program. Children may choose their own partners based on whom they feel comfortable reading with or based on similar topic interests. Or you may decide who would make good pairs. When *you* choose, try all sorts of combinations:

- an emergent reader with a strong reader
- readers similar in their developmental levels
- a talkative child with a talkative child
- a reserved child with a reserved child
- an assertive child with an assertive child
- two children who can read and discuss books in a language other than English
- a native English speaker with a child who is learning English as a second language

Whether you or the students choose the teams, it is important to continually observe them, grouping and regrouping to ensure that they are working together effectively and collaboratively. Partners may read together for several weeks or may change after each book is completed. You may find that, initially, partner reading is easier to manage when partners stick together for a longer period of time. This gives children a chance to develop routines together and get to know each other well.

Children who are learning English as a second language should be permitted to read and discuss some books in their first language. This allows them the benefit of deep understanding of content and fosters their development of proficiency with comprehension strategies. It is well documented that content knowledge and reading strategies transfer from one language to the next. It is also a good idea to pair students who are learning English as a second language with those who are experienced English speakers. Partner reading provides English language learners with meaningful opportunities to read, speak, write, and listen to English. This, along with the individualized

Texts and Reading: Flexible Strategies

Two Readers, Two Books

- Each partner selects a book.
- At the first session, one partner reads his or her book aloud. At the next session, the other partner reads his or her book.
- As an alternative to reading aloud, children may read silently and then do a picture walk for their partners, retelling the stories for fiction or telling about the main ideas for nonfiction.
- This format allows each child to read books written at an appropriate level of difficulty.

Turn Taking with One Book

- Partners select a book together.
- Partners take turns reading aloud. They may switch off every other page or place a marker near the middle of the book, allowing for one child to read the first half and the other to read the second.
- For some children, switching off every other page may be distracting and limit their ability to build meaning across the pages of the text (Taberski 2000). On the other hand, frequent switching may lead children to greater involvement, attention, and assisting behaviors (Griffin 2002). Observe your students carefully to determine how you feel about this practice.

Reading in Unison with One Book

- Partners select a book together.
- Partners read aloud in unison.
- This format provides both children with the opportunity to participate and to develop their reading fluency.

Silent Reading with Two Copies of One Book

- Partners select one book of which there are at least two copies.
- Both partners read silently. After reading a designated number of pages, the partners retell or summarize what has been read so far.
- This practice helps children learn to focus their attention on key content.

Wordless Picture Books

- Children select a book together or each partner selects his or her own book.
- One partner may take full responsibility for "reading" aloud, or partners may work together.
- One option for working together is for each partner to take responsibility for every other page.

Figure 6–2 Texts and Reading: Flexible Strategies

attention and immediate feedback, has shown to enhance both the fluency and the comprehension of second language learners (Krueger and Braun 1998/1999).

Teaching Reading Formats

Teaching children a variety of formats for sharing in the reading will ensure that both partners have ample opportunities to read—both silently and aloud. In teaching the formats, first model the partner reading procedures with one student, and then provide opportunities for child partners to model for the class. Figure 6–2 offers some format possibilities.

On some days, particularly early on, you may wish to assign the whole class to read in a particular format. Modeling formats as you assign them will ensure that the students become familiar with all of the possibilities. Later, allow students to choose their favored formats or to choose on some days.

Many teachers find that when strong decoders are paired with those who are still developing, the team lapses into a pattern in which only the strong decoder does the reading. When you find that certain children are not doing the reading, or when children claim they can't read, you can:

- support them in finding easier or more manageable text to use during partner reading
- suggest that they use a book that they have read in a guided reading group
- suggest that they use a book that you have read to the whole class
- encourage them to *tell* the story or *tell* about the pictures

Continually attempt to promote practices that allow all children to actively participate.

Implementing Team Activities

Partner reading explorations are organized much like literature circle explorations. As with literature circle groups (see Chapter 5), partners may be assigned particular strategies or activities to explore before, during, and after reading. The chart in Figure 6–3 offers ideas for exploring literature through writing, drawing, and talking. As it becomes appropriate, you and teams of children should model new explorations. Observing a few child models before inviting the whole class to engage in an exploration will help you problem solve one step at a time. Figure 6–4 provides an example of a chart that was created

Partner Strategy Explorations

Strategy:	Depending on what is appropriate, partners may engage in the explorations by writing, drawing, or talking.
Predicting and Inferring	• Use the cover to predict what the book will be about (fiction) or to predict what you will learn (nonfiction). As you read, discuss whether your predictions are confirmed. • Do a picture walk to make some predictions about what will happen (fiction) or what you will learn (nonfiction). As you read, discuss whether your predictions are confirmed. • Make an inference based on the cover of the book. As you read, discuss whether your inference is confirmed. • Make an inference about a character/personality.
Purpose Setting	• Do a picture walk to set a purpose for reading. • Decide together on a purpose for reading. After reading, tell how your goals/purposes/hopes were met or not met. • With nonfiction, create a KWL chart (Figure 4–1) or a Gathering Information from Text chart (Figure 4–2). • With fiction, use a story map to focus on and discuss key story elements (see Figures 4–5 to 4–7).
Retelling	• Stop after every few pages to summarize what has happened so far or what you have learned so far. • After reading, synthesize what you have read. • After reading, retell the problem-resolution sequence and tell what you think about it. • After reading, create a story map and use it to retell what you have read (see Figures 4–5 to 4–7). • After reading, use a checklist to retell what you have read (see Figures 6–5 and 6–6). • During and after reading, create an informational text organizer (see Figure 4–8, 4–9, 4–10, 4–21, and 4–22). Use it to retell.
Questioning	• Use sticky notes to record questions you have while reading. • After every three pages, ask your partner a question. • During reading, stop to tell what you wonder about. • After reading, develop a question for the author.
Monitoring	• After every few pages, stop to summarize what you have just read. • After every few pages, tell one thing you have learned. • Stop to talk about words or ideas that confuse you. • Choose three words that you both find interesting. • Find a word that is new to both of you. • Make a record of important or confusing words. • Use sticky notes to code the text together (see Figure 4–12).

Figure 6–3 Partner Strategy Explorations

Visualizing	• During or after reading, draw or tell how you picture a key character or personality.
	• During or after reading, draw or tell how you picture the setting.
	• Choose a picture and reflect on what you might hear, see, smell, taste, and feel from the page.
	• Draw or write about an image you had while reading. Include as many details as possible.
	• Choose any section of text not pictured and describe your mental image.
Connecting	• As you read, use a sticky note to mark something that the text reminds you of (a personal connection). Discuss your connection after reading.
	• As you read, tell about things that surprise you or are new to you.
	• As you read, stop to talk about things that interest you.
	• Discuss a between-text connection.
	• Draw a picture of one character or personality with whom you particularly identified. Compare pictures with your partner.
	• Discuss a connection between something you've read and something you already knew.
Deciding What's Important	• As you read, stop to discuss the main ideas.
	• After reading, create a diagram, picture, or model that shows what you have learned.
	• Choose an important quote or picture. Discuss why it is important.
	• Create an Ideas and Details chart (see Figure 4–21).
	• Create a time line (see Figure 4–22).
	• Use sticky notes to mark interesting text features.
Evaluating	• Decide together on an event you find interesting and discuss what makes it interesting.
	• Find an interesting illustration and discuss what makes it interesting.
	• Tell about a favorite part or a part you didn't like (tell why).
	• Tell about a favorite character or a character you didn't like (tell why).
	• Retell what the main character/personality did and what you would do in a similar situation (tell why).
	• Decide together on an alternative to the resolution.
	• Tell what you think about the illustrations (tell why).
	• Decide on key ways you will use the information you read about.
	• Discuss why you think the author wrote this text.
	• Discuss who you think should read this text (tell why).
	• Discuss how you feel about the author's use of language (tell why).

Figure 6–3 (*Continued*)

Partner Response Ideas

- a part you liked or didn't like

- a web showing what you learned

- a question or wondering

- a story map

- a web showing how you visualized a character

- something you found confusing

- a personal connection

- a connection between what you have read and what we are learning about in school

- a list of interesting words

- a review to share with the class

Figure 6–4 Partner Response Ideas

Checklist for Retelling Stories

Name: _____

I was the: _____ Teller   _____ Observer

The following were included:

___ Title and Author

___ Important Characters

___ Setting

___ Problem or Goal

___ Events

___ Resolution

Goal for next retelling:

Figure 6–5

Checklist for Retelling Informational Text

Name: _____

I was the: _____ Teller   _____ Observer

The following were included:

___ Title and Author

___ Topic and Setting

___ Important Ideas or Events

___ Why Author Wrote This

Goal for next retelling:

Figure 6–6

for a classroom as the students became familiar with response possibilities. Once the responses had been modeled, partners were free to choose their own methods.

Observing, Documenting, and Scaffolding

Regular observation and documentation will help you ensure that partner reading experiences are valuable and that the classroom is running smoothly. To familiarize you with some possibilities for observation and documentation, we'll look at the processes that first-grade teacher Cindy Schultz uses.

Cindy uses partner reading time to document her students' literacy competencies. She visits each pair of readers for a few minutes each day and sometimes observes the class from afar. She usually takes field notes as her students work, but she sometimes fills in information later. Cindy also reserves time for planned one-question interviews. Her goals for the interviews are to understand her students' attitudes toward partner reading, their preferences for partners, and what they value in partners' ways of interacting.

As Cindy collects her data, she draws on her theoretical knowledge of the strategies that effective readers use. She knows what strategies to look for and documents their occurrence. She uses her documentation to reflect on the instruction she might provide, asking herself, What are they doing well? Where could they use help? How are they solving problems? She uses what she learns to help her students build on their strengths and to teach strategies they may not be using. Her plans for instruction always remain open-ended. Because each child and each partner reading situation is unique, Cindy is always adapting her instruction to connect with real classroom needs.

Along with observing and scaffolding individual children, Cindy makes observations that inform whole-class processes. For example, an analysis of her anecdotal notes revealed that some children were rarely chosen as partners—and that when these students were the choosers, the people they chose often expressed disappointment. Cindy recognized that the unchosen children were those who had frequent trouble with relationships; she didn't feel she could help them by merely assigning partners. "What I really wanted," she reflected, "was to begin to change the way the other students felt about [these] children" (Schultz 2000, 49).

Cindy's examples show the importance of continually working to establish a positive and productive learning environment. Partner reading works to its fullest potential when children feel safe reading together and when they understand the discourses for reading and collaborating with another person. As your students grow throughout the year, it will be important to document their progress in ways that enable you (and peers) to provide warm and well-tailored scaffolding. Figures 6–7, 6–8, and 6–9 offer some possibilities for organizing your note taking. Figure 6–10 provides a form to help children learn to self-evaluate.

Valuing Readers

Part of valuing children as human beings is valuing their processes of learning. All children bring to the classroom a wealth of knowledge and experience. This provides their starting point for constructing new knowledge. Partner reading puts children in charge of their learning, allowing them to develop from where they are today. It also shows them that they have something important to contribute to the classroom. As they participate in partner reading activities, they are readers, learners, teachers, collaborators, problem posers, problem solvers, and friends—all roles that contribute to their own growth as well as to the growth of the classroom community.

Class Observation of Partner Reading

List children's names.	I have observed the following students. *Record dates and student strengths.*	Children who need extra support. *Record dates and specific difficulties.*

Figure 6–7

Observing Individual Students During Partner Reading

Place each student's name in a box. Record dates and observations.

Figure 6–8

Detailed Observation of Partner Reading

Child's Name: _____

Dates Observed: _____

Book Titles: _____

_____ Independently reads aloud and/or participates in choral reading.

_____ Expresses thoughts about the text.

_____ Listens to partner's thoughts.

_____ Demonstrates conceptual understandings about the text.

Reading strategies observed during reading or shown through written responses:

____ Predicting   ____ Monitoring

____ Inferring   ____ Visualizing

____ Purpose setting   ____ Connecting

____ Retelling (synthesis or summary)   ____ Deciding what's important

____ Questioning   ____ Monitoring

Notes:

Figure 6–9

Partner Reading Self-Evaluation

Tell one important thing you learned today.

Tell one important way you contributed to your team's discussion.

Tell what you did to be a good listener.

Tell what you could do to make your team work better together.

Figure 6–10

124

RECOMMENDED LITERATURE

English as a Foreign Language Classroom

Gabriela is reading *The Very Hungry Caterpillar* (Carle 1969) to a group of kindergarten students who are learning English as a foreign language. When the caterpillar in the story becomes hungry, Gabriela asks the students to predict what it will eat, and after listening to their ideas, she suggests that they make it their purpose to see if their predictions are confirmed. After reading, the students name the foods the caterpillar ate and discuss their favorite parts of the story. The students then make little books to share the story with other classes in the school. Since they are still learning English, they re-create the story using pictures, and Gabriela takes dictation. As they discuss which pictures to include, and how to sequence them, they use many English words and phrases.

Throughout this book we have seen examples of children and teachers using comprehension strategies to enhance their meaning making. The vignette shows that in one sitting, Gabriela and her students are using several strategies at once. They are *purpose setting*, *inferring*, *monitoring*, *evaluating*, *predicting*, and *retelling*. However, Gabriela focuses her instruction on one strategy at a time. Early in the lesson she focuses on predicting, and after the reading, on retelling. Although readers and listeners must be supported in using several strategies simultaneously, when modeling and discussing the strategies, it is often helpful to focus children's attention on just one at a time. This helps you support them in developing a conscious, or metacognitive, awareness of both the ways in which the strategy works and its relevance to making meaning.

This final chapter provides an annotated bibliography of literature that can be used to introduce and model each of the comprehension strategies described in Chapter 2. The chapter is organized into nine sections, one for each strategy. Along with the book listings, you will find ideas for using them to teach the strategies. In preparation for comprehension instruction in your own classroom, you may find it helpful to start your own collection of books that can be used to teach each strategy.

Books for Teaching Predicting and Inferring

As we have seen, predicting and inferring involve bringing personal knowledge and ideas to text in order to enhance the construction of meaning. In collecting literature to be used for teaching these strategies, almost any text will do as long as your students have some prior knowledge about the content and genre. The more they know about the content and the genre, the more in-depth their predictions and inferences will be and the more sophisticated their strategy use will become. Following are some texts and teaching ideas to be used for teaching predicting and inferring.

Predicting

Predicting using personal experience

Too Many Tamales, **by Gary Soto**

While helping to make tamales for an extended family dinner, Maria surreptitiously tries on her mother's ring. Predictably, it turns up missing. What will Maria do? Will she tell her family before they bite into the tamales or will she search the tamales herself? The Teacher Talk box shows an example of a teacher modeling the use of *personal experience* to predict and think through the answers to such questions.

Teacher Talk: Predicting Using Personal Experience and Knowledge

- Maria realizes the ring is missing. I predict that she'll tell her mom right away to avoid more trouble—I've seen kids do that because they get worried and want to clear things up. Or, she'll try to gently poke through the tamales until she finds the ring—I've also seen people try to hide what they've done if they think it will keep them out of trouble. Let's read on and see.

- As I read, I showed you how I used my own ideas to predict what might happen. Doing this helps me connect my own ideas with what I'm reading and makes the story seem more real for me.

Predicting using world knowledge

Rain Forest, by Helen Cowcher

This fictionalized account of rain forest deforestation shows various creatures living in peace . . . until the rain forest begins to stir and rumble and a sinister scent permeates the air. The author doesn't let the reader know that heavy machinery is causing the disturbance until the middle of the book. Use this text to show students how you can use your *world knowledge* to predict what's coming next (to predict what may be causing the disturbance) and then show them how you confirm or disconfirm your prediction.

Predicting using genre knowledge

The Fat Cat, by Jack Kent

Prediction is often guided by what a reader knows about *genre*. For example, a genre characteristic of traditional stories is a clear problem-resolution sequence. *The Fat Cat* is a Danish folktale about a cat who eats everyone and everything he sees (a problem). As you read, show students how using what you know about story genre helps you predict that there will be a satisfying resolution to this problem.

Predicting using story sequence

The Apple Pie Tree, by Zoe Hall

In *The Apple Pie Tree*, two sisters watch an apple tree change through the seasons. As you read each page, model how you are able to use the *story sequence* to predict what will happen next. Show how both the story line and what you know about trees in general help you predict and construct the text. Discuss with students the ways in which predicting what will come next helps readers connect what they know with the new ideas presented in the text.

Predicting using illustrations

Sense Suspense, by Bruce McMillan

Sense Suspense teaches young readers to use *illustrations* to predict. Each page spread contains a highly magnified close-up of some object that might be viewed, touched, smelled, tasted, or heard—or all of these. Because of the highly magnified view, students must look carefully at the close-ups to predict what they are. After making the predictions, a regular-size view of each object allows students to confirm or disconfirm their predictions.

Predicting using cover features

Chickens Aren't the Only Ones, by Ruth Heller

Cover features also help readers make predictions. The title of *Chickens Aren't the Only Ones* raises an interesting question: Chickens aren't the only ones to do what? The back cover lets the reader know that chickens aren't the only ones to lay eggs. After examining the cover features, work with students to make a list of the animals they predict they will read about. During the reading, discuss whether their predictions were confirmed or disconfirmed. Add to the list any creatures that were missed to emphasize for children how reading leads to new understandings.

Predicting using knowledge about characters and settings

More Than Anything Else, by Marie Bradby

Prior knowledge about the characters and/or setting of a book also helps readers make predictions. *More Than Anything Else* tells of a young Booker T. Washington's longing to learn to read. (Washington was born a slave in 1856, when it was illegal for slaves to read and write; nine years later, the Emancipation Proclamation was read to the slaves on the tobacco plantation on which he lived.) Show students how you use what you know about the characters and setting to guide your predictions. For example, "The cover of this book shows a picture of a young boy looking at a book. This boy is Booker T. Washington, and he was born a slave. Knowing that it was illegal for slaves to read and write, I am going to make a prediction about the meaning of the title. I predict that Booker wants to learn to *read* more than anything else."

Predicting using text features

Protecting Endangered Species, by Felicity Brooks

The features in a text can be very helpful in making predictions about what will be learned. *Protecting Endangered Species* describes the plight of plants and animals that are in danger of extinction and offers solutions for preserving them. This book is rich in *text features*, including headings, illustrations, captions, and fonts. As you take a text walk before reading, show students how you can use text features to make predictions about what you will learn, and discuss with them how such activity helps you prepare for the reading.

Inferring

Inferring using personal experience

McDuff Moves In, by Rosemary Wells

Children's *personal experiences* contribute greatly to the inferences they make. Personal experiences are the substance for filling in information and ideas that the author does not state explicitly. In *McDuff Moves In*, a small dog (named McDuff) tumbles out of a dogcatcher's truck and finds temporary shelter in a kind couple's home. After feeding and bathing the dog, the couple head for the dog pound, but then change their minds and turn around and take the dog back home. As you read, model your way of using personal experience to inform your inferences. The Teacher Talk box shows an example.

Teacher Talk

- I can infer that McDuff must have felt confused and unhappy when he tumbled out of the truck and didn't really have a place to go. I adopted my dog from a family when she was already a year old. At first, she wouldn't eat and she seemed so sad. When the family came to visit her after a few days, she seemed to want to go get in their car and go back home.
- When I infer like this, do you see how it helps me *feel* the story better?

Inferring using world knowledge

The Great Kapok Tree, by Lynne Cherry

Children also use *knowledge about the world beyond their personal lives* to infer. *The Great Kapok Tree* is the story of a community of rain forest animals who face the potential loss of the tree in which they live. The cover shows a man with an axe looking at a tree. The cover and narrative may be used to model for children how you infer using your world knowledge:

What can we infer will happen?

129

What can we infer that this man is thinking?

What makes us think so?

What can we infer happens to animals who live in such trees?

Given what we know about the rain forest, what are the broader consequences for our planet?

Why do you think the author may have written this book?

How does inferring help us understand and see this story in new ways?

Inferring using illustrations

***The Dinosaurs of Waterhouse Hawkins*, by Barbara Kerley**

Illustrations are the source of many reading inferences. *The Dinosaurs of Waterhouse Hawkins* is the true story of an author, artist, and lecturer who was a pioneer in helping humans understand the world of dinosaurs. The illustrations in this book are particularly useful in teaching children about inferring. A prereading picture walk leads the reader to infer that the narrative begins when Waterhouse is a boy and ends after his death. Some illustrations allow the reader to infer feelings: one shows Waterhouse in his museum engaged in a toast; another shows a proud Waterhouse displaying his work for a crowd. Some illustrations are translucent, leading the reader to infer that ideas, rather than realities, are being presented. As you read, show your students how thinking through the pictures gives you background knowledge about what you are about to read and helps you understand the text more deeply.

Inferring using the title

***Log Hotel*, by Anne Schreiber**

Book titles also lead to inferences. *Log Hotel* shows what happens as an oak log decomposes in the forest. The Teacher Talk box shows a way to use the title of this book to teach about inferring.

> ## Teacher Talk: Inferring Using Titles and Illustrations
>
> - What can be inferred from the title *Log Hotel*? Why do you think the author chose to name the book *Log Hotel*?
> - As we turn through the pages, are your inferences about the title confirmed or disconfirmed?

Inferring about characters

No, David! by David Shannon

Many of a reader's inferences are about *characters*—their feelings, intentions, motivations, and actions. Making inferences about characters helps readers connect with and understand them better. *No, David!* is a fun little story about a young boy named David who tracks mud on the floor, writes on the wall, plays with his food, and runs naked down the street. The cover shows David tipping over the fishbowl. Use both the title and the illustrations to discuss what can be inferred about this little boy (he is curious; inquisitive; energetic; mischievous).

Inferring about themes

The Table Where Rich People Sit, by Byrd Baylor

Theme is a story element that must be inferred. In *The Table Where Rich People Sit*, a young girl who feels that her family is deficient because they are too poor learns a new definition for *rich*. What really matters, she discovers, is the beautiful life her family lives. This book's obvious but unstated theme makes it ideal for teaching children to infer. The Teacher Talk box provides examples of the kinds of questions that prompt children to consider a story's theme.

Teacher Talk: Inferring About Themes

- What important lesson did the character learn?
- What important lesson did the author want me to learn? Is there a message that the author wants me to pick up?
- What big reason might the author have had for writing this book?

Inferring about events

Ibis: A True Whale Story, by John Himmelman

This book tells the story of a young humpback whale who becomes caught in a fishing net. The Teacher Talk box shows examples of the kind of teacher language that supports inferring about events.

Teacher Talk: General Inferring

- Ibis hears a humming noise and looks up to see something dark passing overhead. What can you infer she is seeing?

> • When Ibis becomes caught in the net, what can you infer will happen? When she breaks free, but continues to live with her mouth and tail still wrapped in netting, what can you infer will happen?

Books for Teaching Purpose Setting

When selecting literature for teaching children about purpose setting, choose topics that appeal to your students and/or topics that connect in some way with your curriculum. As you model, it is important that you have an authentic purpose for reading, be it purely for pleasure or to meet more specific learning goals. Authenticity of purpose will help children understand the usefulness of this strategy.

Reading for general information (nonfiction)

The Magic School Bus: Inside Ralphie: A Book About Germs, **by Joanna Cole**

Often, we read nonfiction with a general purpose of learning something new about a topic. We set purposes to help us achieve this goal. For example, *Inside Ralphie* takes the reader through a young boy's bloodstream, showing how germs make him sick and how his body works to make him well again. Modeling how you read the book for the purpose of *pulling out general information* related to these two concepts will help your students learn to set purposes and also learn something important about health. As you gather the information, consider using a KWL chart (Figure 4–1), a Gathering Information form (Figure 4–2), an exposition web (Figure 4–9), or an Ideas and Details chart (Figure 4–21).

Reading for specific information (nonfiction)

Desert Babies, **by Kathy Darling**

Rain Forest Babies, **by Kathy Darling**

At other times, we read nonfiction to meet more *specific goals*, and often we do not need to read an entire text in order to achieve these goals. For example, Kathy Darling's books introduce a variety of animals that live in the wild. Each animal is allotted a two-page spread that includes pictures, a narrative containing high-interest information, and a list of facts about the animal. Examining the text features allows the reader to read just for the desired information. The Teacher Talk box offers examples of the kind of language used to model this strategy.

Teacher Talk: Using Format to Set and Meet Purposes

- My purpose for reading _Desert Babies_ is to learn more about what desert animals eat. I'm going to focus on that as I read.
- So far, I've read about two of the animals in this book: camels and caracals. As I was reading, I noticed that the author wrote some interesting information about each animal in the first section, and then used this yellow, boxed-in section to give a list of facts, including information about favorite foods. I predict that she'll do the same thing with a different animal on the next page. Since we're looking mostly for what desert animals eat, I can meet my purpose by going right to the boxed-in section to find out.

Using knowledge about genre to read for general information

A Picture Book of Harriet Tubman, **by David Adler**

Often, _genre_ is used to help set and meet purposes for reading. The Teacher Talk box shows an example of a teacher using the biography genre to help set his purpose.

Teacher Talk: Purpose Setting Using Genre

- This biography describes some important events in Harriet Tubman's life.
- When I read a biography, I make it my purpose to do two things. First, I learn as much as I can about the person. Second, I learn as much as I can about the times.
- I don't know much about Harriet Tubman, but I know that a good biography will give me information about these two things.
- After I read, I will want to talk with you about what I've learned about Harriet Tubman and about the times in which she lived. This will help me to be sure I have met my reading goals.

Using knowledge about genre to read for specific information

Happy Birthday, Martin Luther King, **by Jean Marzollo**

A Picture Book of Martin Luther King, Jr., **by David Adler**

These two books present biographical information about Martin Luther King. As with the previous example, they may be used to model how knowledge of genre helps readers achieve their goals. However, here the focus is different. Sometimes, rather than collecting information in general, we are looking only for a particular bit of information. The Teacher Talk box provides an example.

> ### Teacher Talk: Purpose Setting to Meet a Specific Goal
>
> - Because we've been studying important people in history, I know a lot about Martin Luther King's work. But I don't know very much about his childhood. I'm going to skim through these books to see if I can find out about his early life. I'll start at the beginning because usually, biographies are presented in time order.
> - Thinking about my purpose helps me read for just the information I need.

Reading to develop insight into particular concepts

The Other Side, **by Jacqueline Woodson**

Often, we use purpose setting to help children develop insight into particular *concepts or curricular themes*, such as race relations, family relations, friendship, sharing, social activism, environmental activism, or good versus evil. *The Other Side* is a story about an African American girl's relations with her European American neighbor and how these relations change over time. Setting a specific purpose for reading a book like this helps children focus on developing particular understandings. For example, "We have been reading this text set on race relations. Here's another book addressing that issue. Let's read this book to see what else we can learn about race relations."

Sharing information with others

> *Sally Ann Thunder Ann Whirlwind Crockett*, by Steven Kellogg: The tale of an American legend known for her prodigious ability to outdo any person or creature who crossed her path.
>
> *John Henry*, by Julius Lester: The tale of an American legend of amazing strength and spirit.

Swamp Angel, by Anne Isaacs: The tale of a great American woodswoman.

Johnny Appleseed, by Steven Kellogg: The tale of a hero of the American frontier.

Sometimes, text is read purely for pleasure and it is enjoyable for children to *retell* what they have read. As you read the traditional tales listed here, show students how you prepare for a retelling by making it your purpose to pull out key ideas and details. Figures 4–3, 4–5, and 4–7 may help you to do so. (Keep in mind that children also enjoy retelling parts of *nonfiction* texts. See Chapter 4 for ideas related to retelling nonfiction.)

Using cover illustrations to find a way into the reading

Abuela, **by Arthur Dorros**

The *cover illustrations* on books often give clues to what the text will be about and can help readers set a purpose that will bring them into the reading. For example, the cover of *Abuela* shows a young girl (Rosalba) and a woman (her *abuela*) holding hands as they fly over a city. Thinking about and discussing cover illustrations is a way to set initial purposes for the reading. For example, "Let's see if we can find out what these two characters are up to."

Using the title to find a way into the reading

How the Birds Got Their Colours: An Aboriginal Story, **retold by Pamela Lofts**

Many books have *titles* that are suggestive of their content. Setting a reading purpose based on the title can help children begin to focus and tune in to the author's goals or meanings. Model how you use informative titles to set an initial purpose for reading: "Some books have titles that help us know what to focus on. Let's read this book to find out how birds got their colors."

Books for Teaching Retelling

Probably the most important reason to teach retelling is that it helps children reflect on, rethink, and reconsider what they have read. As you teach, keep in mind that retelling can take the form of both summary (a detailed sketch) and synthesis (a statement capturing the gist) (see Chapter 2). This section addresses retelling with fiction first and then nonfiction.

Retelling with Fiction

In collecting fiction to teach retelling, look for stories that have a logical sequence and clear story structure. For example, *The Three Billy Goats Gruff* and *The Three Little Pigs* are sequenced in terms of first, second, and third, and both of their structures involve easy-to-identify characters, settings, problems, and resolutions. The logical sequence and clear structure give the reteller clues to remember what's next. Familiar tales with a new twist work well, too. For example, *Lon Po Po* is a Red Riding Hood story from China. Knowing the North American version of the tale helps the teller structure the recounting of new versions. Finally, whenever possible, use books that relate to your content area curriculum in some way.

Figure 7–1 offers a set of general retelling ideas and experiences that may be tailored to fit any of the fiction selections that follow. As you use these ideas, remember that the activities should be aimed at helping children develop retelling as a comprehension strategy, rather than solely as a way for you to assess their comprehension.

> *Goldilocks and the Three Bears*, by James Marshall: The traditional tale told in a very humorous way.
> *The Three Billy Goats Gruff*, by Paul Galdone: Three clever billy goats outsmart the troll who lives under the bridge.
> *The Rough-Face Girl*, by Rafe Martin: An Algonquin Cinderella tale.
> *Mufaro's Beautiful Daughters*, by John Steptoe: A Cinderella story inspired by an African folktale.
> *Lon Po Po*, by Ed Young: A Red Riding Hood story from China.
> *The Three Little Pigs*, by Paul Galdone: The three little pigs go head-to-head with the crafty wolf.
> *The True Story of the 3 Little Pigs!* by John Scieska: The traditional tale told from the perspective of the wolf.
> *Gingerbread Baby*, by Jan Brett: A gingerbread baby jumps out of the oven and is chased all over town.
> *The Tale of the Mandarin Ducks*, by Katherine Paterson: A Japanese kitchen maid releases a beautiful mandarin duck that has been caged by a greedy lord.
> *The Secret Footprints*, by Julia Alvarez: An enchanting legend (with Dominican roots) about the *ciguapas*, whose toes point behind them.

Retelling with Nonfiction

In collecting nonfiction to teach retelling, choose books that connect to your content area curriculum. Figure 7–2 offers a set of general

---

Retelling Fiction

- During reading, pause to discuss or think about what you have read so far.

- During reading, retell what you have read after every few pages. Either summarize or synthesize.

- Retell a story to a friend (see Figure 4–3).

- Reenact a part of a story with a small group.

- Make puppets to retell a story.

- Draw or sculpt a retelling.

- Collect a set of props to retell with.

- Retell into a tape recorder.

- Create a story map to retell (see Figures 4–5, 4–6, and 4–7).

Figure 7–1 Retelling Fiction

prompts that may be tailored to fit any of the nonfiction selections that follow (or any other nonfiction text).

> *A Picture Book of Jesse Owens*, by David Adler: A biography of Jesse Owens, Olympic champion in track and field.
> *Purple Mountain Majesties*, by Barbara Younger: The life story of Katherine Bates, author of *America the Beautiful*.
> *Apples*, by Gail Gibbons: A chronological history of apples in the United States followed by a description of how an apple develops through the seasons.
> *Red Leaf, Yellow Leaf*, by Lois Ehlert: A description of the development of a sugar maple tree.
> *What's Inside? My Body*, by Angela Royston: A description of body parts including the chest, head, and stomach.
> *Why Frogs Are Wet*, by Judy Hawes: Factual information about frogs.
> *Sharks*, by Seymour Simon: Factual information about sharks.

Books for Teaching Questioning

In preparing to model and teach questioning strategies, look for literature that will inspire children's curiosity and wonderings or that they

---

Retelling Nonfiction

- During reading, pause to discuss or think about what you have read so far.

- During reading, retell what you have read after every few pages. Either summarize or synthesize.

- As you read, jot down the key ideas.

- Retell a part of the text to a friend (see Figure 4–4).

- Reenact a part of the text with a small group.

- Make puppets to retell a part of the text.

- Draw or sculpt a retelling.

- Collect a set of props to retell with.

- Retell into a tape recorder.

- Create a web or map to retell (see Figures 4–8, 4–9, and 4–10).

- Consider what kind of graphic organizer could help you to retell a part of this text (see Figure 2–4).

Figure 7–2 Retelling Nonfiction

will find puzzling or complex in some way. As you teach, keep in mind that children must be encouraged to ask questions about what they read, not just to answer them. Effective readers ask questions all the time, both to understand the text more deeply and to organize their thinking.

Questioning within the text

Tough Boris, **by Mem Fox**

Tough Boris is a story that can be used to show children how *questioning within the text* helps readers dig in to what they are reading in order to experience it more deeply. Questioning within the text involves the reader in reflecting on questions that relate directly to the text but not necessarily to wider issues. In *Tough Boris*, main character Boris von der Borch seems to be a hardened old pirate—or is he? Even though Boris is described as massive, scruffy, greedy, and scary, his esteemed parrot rides on his shoulder as he travels the high seas. When the parrot dies, Tough Boris cries, raising an interesting question: What kind of person is Boris, really? What techniques does the author use to create complexity in this character?

But that's not the whole story. The illustrations feature a little boy with a violin who is not mentioned in the narrative. Only a close and thoughtful viewing of the illustrations will shed light on the rest of the ideas contained in this book. As you read, show children how you examine intriguing illustrations to heighten your understanding of the story: What is this little boy doing across the pages of the book? What is his relationship with Boris? Why did the author choose to tell this part of the story through pictures only? Questioning within the text—through examining both the narrative and the illustrations—helps children move deeply into text and appreciate its complexities and intricacies.

Questioning beyond the text

Roses Sing on New Snow, by Paul Yee

Sometimes, children's questioning goes beyond the text itself, serving as a tool for them to reflect on wider issues. *Roses Sing on New Snow* is set in turn-of-the-century Chinatown, where Maylin cooks fine food for her father's restaurant. However, her lazy brothers are given all the credit. When the visiting governor of South China wants the brothers to demonstrate the preparation of a particularly delicious dish, the brothers rush to Maylin for a list of ingredients and a demonstration. Even with her direction, the dish is just not the same. When the governor himself seeks instruction from Maylin, his cooking, too, results in a less-than-satisfactory dish. Maylin explains, "If you and I sat down with paper and brush and black ink, could we bring forth identical paintings?" The Teacher Talk box offers some possibilities for modeling questioning that requires *thinking beyond the text*.

Teacher Talk: Questioning Beyond the Text

- Why do you think Maylin's father gives her brothers credit for the cooking?
- Why do you think the brothers' and the governor's dishes do not taste as good as Maylin's?
- What might Maylin mean when she says, "If you and I sat down with paper and brush and black ink, could we bring forth identical paintings?"
- Where could we find the answers to these questions?

Questions about words

The Sign in Mendel's Window, **by Mildred Phillips**

Children often have questions about *specific words* they encounter in text. In cases in which the meaning of a word is not crucial to understanding, it is acceptable to simply read on. In cases in which word meanings are crucial, children must use vocabulary strategies. *The Sign in Mendel's Window* is an ideal text for teaching children to use context clues to determine word meanings. Set in a small European village, the story opens with Mendel the butcher hanging a FOR RENT sign that raises the eyebrows of the friendly village neighbors. Have Mendel and Molly struck it rich? Why is the butcher shop for rent? In response to the villagers' questions, Mendel responds, "So many questions . . . If only questions were zloty!" The clues to the meaning of *zloty* and other fun words (such as *groszy, scoundrel, scalding,* and *snickered*) are found throughout the text, making it ideal for teaching children to use context clues to determine word meanings. A set of vocabulary strategies is listed in Figure 4–14.

Questions about genre

Raven: A Trickster Tale from the Pacific Northwest, **by Gerald McDermott**

There are times when considering questions about *genre* can enhance a child's understanding of text. Raven is a central figure in many Native American trickster tales across the Pacific Northwest. In this tale, he finds a way to bring light to a world of people living in darkness and cold. The Teacher Talk box shows examples of how considering questions about genre can help children understand a text more deeply.

Teacher Talk: Questioning About Genre

- What is a trickster tale?
- What usually happens in a trickster tale?
- How does Raven fit the role of a trickster?
- How do Raven's tricks compare with those of other tricksters we've read about?
- Do you believe that this trickster tale really happened? Why? If not, do you think that some people believe this tale really happened? Why?
- How can thinking about these questions better help us understand the trickster tales we read?

Questions about language

This Big Sky, by Pat Mora

This book of short poems celebrates the beauty of the American Southwest. Pat Mora's use of imagery, metaphor, and analogy provoke many interesting questions that help the reader dig deeply into the meaning of the poetry. For example, to enhance understanding, a reader might take the time to consider the following questions about *language*:

> What is the meaning of "whispers of giant pines"?
>
> What is a "thorny silence"?
>
> What images come to mind when the author describes the wind as having "hot breath" or an old woman's skirt as being the color of "the lavender of rain clouds"?
>
> Why might the author have chosen "Joyful Jabber" as a title for the poem about jays?

Questions about special illustrations and text features

Martin's Big Words, by Doreen Rappaport

This book about the life of Martin Luther King has the potential to raise numerous questions—because of both its *illustrations* and its *special features*. For example, when opening the book, the reader finds a two-page spread of stained-glass windows. The next illustration contains a sign reading WHITE ONLY. Subsequent pages show images of churches, a bus, protests, the American Flag, and more. Speculating on the reasons for the illustrations sheds light on the content of the book and helps readers understand the text more deeply.

In terms of features, the text contains several quotations presented in large, colored fonts. For example, "Hate cannot drive out hate. Only love can do that." "When the history books are written, someone will say there lived black people who had the courage to stand up for their rights." "I have a dream that one day in Alabama little black boys and black girls will join hands with little white boys and white girls as sisters and brothers." Paying attention to these special features will help the reader develop insight into the context of Martin Luther King's life and into his goals and dreams for a better world. It will also help children develop insight into the author's craft. As you read with children, show them how asking questions about illustrations and text features can help them see text ideas through a new lens.

Answering questions using dictionaries and encyclopedias

Often, children have questions whose answers can be found in dictionaries or encyclopedias. To use these materials effectively, children need to know why and how they are used. This takes many on-the-spot experiences in which questions are answered as they arise within the context of real inquiries. Regularly model how you use children's dictionaries and encyclopedias to answer specific questions about a topic.

Reading with a questioning stance

The Reason for a Flower, by Ruth Heller

We want children to know that questioning is a normal part of reading. Model for children the questions that arise in your daily reading. Starting with the title, *The Reason for a Flower* has the potential to raise questions in the mind of the reader. The Teacher Talk box offers some examples.

Teacher Talk: Questioning

- The title of this book is *The Reason for a Flower*. Before I begin to read, I already have a question about the title. What are the good reasons for a flower? I'll be sure to pay attention to answering that as I read.
- I've just read about pollen, but I still don't understand what pollen does for a flower. How do these ideas fit together? I wonder where I can find the answer to this new question that has emerged from my reading.
- Now that I've finished reading, what have I learned about the reasons for flowers?

Questioning and question-answer relationships using KWL

Titanic, by Victoria Sherrow

An historical account of the "unsinkable" ship, *Titanic* is an excellent book for using a KWL chart (Figure 4–1) to teach questioning strategies. First, show your students how a KWL chart can help them organize questions. Use the K column to think about what you know about the Titanic, and the W column to record your questions. As you read, document the answers to your questions (and other things you learn) in the L column.

KWL processes provide opportunities to discuss *question-answer relationships* as well. The Teacher Talk box shows examples.

> ## Teacher Talk: Question-Answer Relationships
>
> - How could I find the answer to this first question on my KWL chart?
> - Is the answer in the text? [How many people were aboard the Titanic? How many seats were available on the lifeboats?]
> - Do I have to put together different parts of the text to answer it? [What was the voyage like after the captain knew the ship was going to sink?]
> - Do I have to use my background knowledge along with text information? [What must have been going through the minds of the last people on the sinking ship?]
> - Do I even need the text to answer the question? [How do people in the world react when they hear of disasters?]

Using text features to answer specific questions

Amazing Animal Disguises, **by Sandie Sowler**

This fascinating book about the ways in which animals protect themselves makes use of numerous *text features*: a table of contents, an index, headings, illustrations, and captions. Such texts are useful for modeling ways of using text features to get specific questions answered. For example, if you are interested in learning about imitation or mimicry, the table of contents tells you where to look. If you want to learn about specific creatures such as polar bears or zebras, the index helps. A quick skim through the headings and illustrations gives you an overall picture of the content. Modeling these strategies for your students shows them how text features foster efficient reading.

Books for Teaching Monitoring

Monitoring involves keeping track of meaning and knowing when and how to address confusions when they arise. In choosing texts for modeling monitoring strategies, look for those that your students will find somewhat challenging in terms of content.

General monitoring strategies

Osa's Pride, **by Ann Grifalconi**

Osa's grandmother tells a story about pride that helps Osa come to a new understanding of herself. The Teacher Talk box shows an example of a teacher using this book to teach children about general monitoring processes.

Teacher Talk

- I'm going to show you how I focus on monitoring my understanding as I read. Monitoring helps us to be sure we understand what is read and to make sense of parts that are unclear.

- The narrative begins with, "When I was no bigger than a coffee bush I learned something amazing about myself that had to do with broken eggs, blue cloth, and foolish pride!" After reading this first page, I already know who is telling this story. This story is told *by* Osa, one of the characters. When I *monitor*, I'm making sure I know what's happening in the story.

- There's something else important on this first page. The author gives me a clue about what to pay attention to: she says that Osa learned something amazing about herself. As I read, I'm going to be sure to look for what that amazing thing is. Do you see how monitoring can help me set little goals as I read?

- *Pride* . . . this seems to be an important word in this story. The author has used it a few times, and it appears on the book jacket. I've heard this word before, but let's say I'm still figuring out what it means. To figure out the meaning, I'm going to really think about what I know about this word, and I'm going to pay attention to what it means to the author. Sometimes monitoring involves making sure we understand important words.

- I'm going to pause right here to summarize for myself what I've read so far. This will help me to be sure I am following the story line. Probably the most important part of monitoring is being sure I have understood what I have read so far.

- When I read this part for the first time, I was a little confused. The grandma says, "If we could only see ourselves, Osa! We would all be so much happier." I had to really think about what this meant. I decided that this was a creative use of language, like we have listed on our Fix-Up Strategies chart (see Figure 2–3). The grandma didn't mean we couldn't see ourselves in a mirror, she meant that we don't see how our actions affect other people. Part of monitoring involves doing something about the little confusions that arise as we read.

- Now that I've finished reading, I want to think back to a purpose I set early on. Have I discovered the amazing thing that Osa has learned about herself?

Monitoring illustrations

So Far from the Sea, by Eve Bunting

In *So Far from the Sea*, a young family visits Manzanar, a Japanese internment camp in California where the father character was held as a boy during World War II. This story presents an interesting opportunity for helping students learn to monitor their *understandings of illustrations*. The illustrations go back and forth between color and black and white to depict scenes from the present and the past. As you read, show children how you take the time to examine the illustrations and think about the meanings that the illustrator is trying to convey.

Monitoring by tracking the sequence of events

Follow the Drinking Gourd, by Jeanette Winter

One important way to monitor understanding is to periodically *rethink the sequence of events*. Any book with a clear sequence of events will work for modeling this strategy. For example, *Follow the Drinking Gourd* tells the story of a group of slaves who face various tribulations as they make their way toward freedom. As you model, show students how you focus on key ideas that will help you track the story line, rather than rethinking every detail.

Monitoring by tracking story elements

Train to Somewhere, by Eve Bunting

Train to Somewhere is the story of a group of 1870s orphan children, each of whom is placed with a family while riding across the country on a train. In monitoring, children may find it helpful to track their comprehension by focusing on *key story elements*. With this in mind, as you model, you might ask questions such as the following:

- Who are the *characters*? How does this character develop and change over time?
- What do I know about the *setting* and how does this help me understand the story?
- What major *problem* does the main character face?
- What contributes to the character *resolving* this problem?
- Have I identified the *theme*?

Monitoring through summary and synthesis

I Wonder Why I Blink and Other Questions About My Body, by Brigid Avison

Summarizing and *synthesizing* can be helpful strategies for monitoring comprehension. Each page of *I Wonder Why I Blink* begins with a question and answer about the human body. Show students how you monitor your understandings by briefly rethinking (summarizing or synthesizing) what you have learned from each page.

Addressing confusions

Sea Lion Roars, **by Drew Lamm**

Along with keeping track of what they are reading, it is important that children become familiar with *fix-up strategies* that help them address confusions that arise while reading. Some common fix-up strategies include

- rereading
- reading on
- reading more slowly to clarify confusion
- looking carefully at the illustrations
- thinking about the use of punctuation
- identifying and determining the meaning of any confusing words

To teach fix-up strategies (see Figure 2–3 for a more detailed list), choose any text that contains vocabulary or concepts that your students are likely to find challenging or complex. Try to model just one or two fix-ups at a time so that you can thoroughly explain their significance. For example, *Sea Lion Roars* is the fictionalized story of a sea lion who becomes tangled in a fishing net. The text contains complex but relevant vocabulary such as *kelp, forage, rookery, petrel,* and *ferry*, making it a good choice for teaching children to determine the meaning of unknown words. Some of the words in the text are easily defined by the surrounding context and the illustrations; others are more easily defined by using the glossary at the end of the book.

Coding

Sea Turtles, by Caroline Arnold: A nonfiction narrative that teaches all about the lives of sea turtles.
Solar System, by Gregory Vogt: A book of facts and photographs about our solar system.

Coding is another technique that fosters monitoring. Show children how you use coding (see Figure 4–12) to monitor your understandings as you read a variety of kinds of text. For example, parts of *Sea Turtles* might be coded with + + (I can use this for my project), or ☺☺ (Discuss this part with group), or ?? (I don't understand this part). *Solar System* might be coded with **NEW** (I didn't know this before) or

WEB (Add this information to web on asteroids). Possibilities for coding are endless.

Books for Teaching Visualizing

Visualization helps readers connect with text as they consider the sensory images evoked by the characters, settings, and events. To teach visualizing, choose literature that activates children's senses. Typical visualization prompts include

- In your mind, what do the characters or personalities look like?
- What does the setting look like?
- Think about the smells and tastes that might be present.
- What sounds do you think could be heard at this point?
- Think about anything that could be touched or felt. What does it feel like?

Visualizing with wordless picture books

Deep in the Forest, by Brinton Turkle

Wordless picture books provide excellent opportunities to visualize using all of the senses. In *Deep in the Forest*, a bear sneaks into a family's cottage, tasting the porridge, trying out the chairs, and playing on the beds. To show children how visualization helps readers experience a story, think aloud about what this Goldilocks-like bear might smell, see, taste, touch, and feel while she is in the cottage and about how she might appear as the story progresses and comes to a climax.

Visualizing with fiction

Owl Moon, by Jane Yolen

Come On, Rain! by Karen Hesse

In *Owl Moon*, late on a winter night, a child and father go owling. Jane Yolen's writing is rich in the kind of description that stimulates visualization: the moon is bright, a train whistle blows, dogs howl, the air is chilly, the shadows are black, the snow is whiter than milk, and an owl calls. *Come On, Rain!* tells the story of an unbearably sizzling hot day, on which a young girl waits for the rain to fall. The narrative is rich with visual and other sensory descriptions. For example, before it rains, "heat wavers off tar patches in the broiling alleyway . . . the smell of hot tar and garbage bullies the air . . . sweat trickles . . ." and iced tea is served. Help children live texts by supporting them in carefully considering the author's words and using them to imagine the children's experiences.

Visualizing with poetry

Pass It On: African American Poetry for Children, **selected by Wade Hudson**

The Earth Under Sky Bear's Feet: Native American Poems of the Land, **by Joseph Bruchac and Thomas Locker**

The Great Frog Race and Other Poems, **by Kristine O'Connell George**

Poetry is an ideal genre for teaching children to visualize. The three books cited here contain many poems with rich, descriptive language that leads to rich visual images. To model visualization with poetry, choose your favorites. Read them aloud to children several times, thinking aloud about your personal images, and the ways in which they enhance your understandings, connections, and enjoyment of the pieces.

Visualizing with nonfiction

Escape from the Ice, **by Connie and Peter Roop**

This nonfiction book tells the riveting story of an expedition into the Antarctic led by Sir Ernest Shackleton. When Shackleton's ship becomes icebound, the ordinary expedition turns into a harsh and chilling struggle for survival. Use visualization throughout the reading to help students gain a sense of what the survivors experienced: the feel of ice-cold winds, the intense hunger, the sights of the Antarctic wilderness, and the tensions of struggling to survive.

Visualizing with a memoir

26 Fairmount Avenue, **by Tomie DePaola**

In this memoir, well-loved author Tomie DePaola tells stories of his early childhood about the building of a new home, relationships with grandparents, a trip to the movies, the first day of school, and more. Use visualization to help children relive what Tomie experienced in the 1930s through all of the senses. For example, in Chapter 3, when Tomie goes to the movies, he is treated to "little chewy licorice candies." In Chapter 6, when family and friends set out to clear the backyard of the new house, things get frighteningly hot and smoky, but Tomie's mother saves the day by spraying all with the water hose.

Visualizing with photographs

Shades of Black: A Celebration of Our Children, **by Sandra L. Pinkney**

Shades of Black contains lively photographs accompanied by rich descriptions of the varied shades and tones of black children's skin and eyes and the varied textures and lengths of black children's hair: "I am the velvety orange in a peach and the coppery brown in a pretzel . . . My hair is the soft puffs in a cotton ball and the stiff ringlets in lambs wool . . . " With this book, try reading aloud the descriptions and asking children to visualize before showing the photographs. This process helps children tune in to the language of description and use it to enhance their meaning making.

Visualizing with a biography

Crazy Horse's Vision, by Joseph Bruchac: A fictionalized biography of the early years of a great Lakota leader.
George Washington: A Picture Book Biography, by James Cross Giblin: A biography of America's first president.
Eleanor, by Barbara Cooney: A biography of Eleanor Roosevelt's childhood.
Minty: A Story of Young Harriet Tubman, by Alan Schroeder: A fictionalized view of what life was like for Harriet Tubman, one of North America's great heroines.

Visualization is a useful technique for helping students adventure into the worlds of the historical personalities about whom they read. As you read these books with children, think aloud about how the subjects and their surroundings might look and about what they might see, hear, smell, touch, and feel.

Books for Teaching Connecting

Personal Connections

To teach children about making personal connections, choose books that contain events, experiences, and ideas that could be considered universal to many of your students. Keep in mind that the goal of teaching this strategy is not simply to get children to connect but also to get them to use connecting as a way to build understanding. The Teacher Talk box shows a set of general questions that may be tailored to fit any of the book selections that follow.

Teacher Talk: Questions for Personal Connections

- What feelings or experiences have you had that are like those of the characters or personalities in this book?
- In what ways are you like or different from this character or personality?
- Do these characters remind you of anybody you know?

- Have you been to a place like this?
- Have you ever done something like this?
- Have you ever seen something like this?
- What do you know about this already?
- How does connecting help you understand what you read?

Peter's Chair, by Ezra Jack Keats: Peter's life changes when his sister is born.

Boundless Grace, by Mary Hoffman: Grace's father, who lives in Africa, wants Grace to come and visit—and meet his new family.

The Lion's Whiskers, by Ann Grifalconi: In this Ethiopian folktale, Fanaye marries a widower with a young son. The new mother-son relationship is strained at first, but Fanaye finds the key to making it work.

It's Mine! by Leo Lionni: A fable in which three frogs initially look out only for themselves but then learn a valuable lesson about cooperation and sharing.

Yoko, by Rosemary Wells: Yoko's classmates make fun of her lunch.

Chrysanthemum, by Kevin Henkes: Chrysanthemum loves her name . . . until the other kids tease her about it.

Lilly's Purple Plastic Purse, by Kevin Henkes: Lilly loves her teacher . . . until she brings her purple plastic purse to school and cannot wait to show it.

David Goes to School, by David Shannon: When David goes to school, he raises chaos for all.

Meet Danitra Brown, by Nikki Grimes: A series of poems about Danitra Brown, who experiences what many children experience: she gets teased, helps her mom while she is sick, pretends to be a star, consoles a friend, forgives a friend, goes "bike crazy," tells stories, and more.

The Lemon Drop Jar, by Christine Widman: A young girl visits her Great Aunt Emma, who shares a special family story about a treasured lemon drop jar.

Tell Me a Story, Mama, by Angela Johnson: The mother of a young child shares memories from her childhood.

How Kids Grow, by Jean Marzollo: An account of the accomplishments and favored activities of children from birth to seven.

Something to Remember Me By, by Susan Bosak with Laurie McGaw: The story of a grandmother and her granddaughter, told across their years together.

When Winter Comes, by Robert Maass; *When Spring Comes*, by Robert Maass; *When Summer Comes*, by Robert Maass; *When Autumn Comes*, by Robert Maass: Robert Maass' books provide photographic and narrative accounts of children engaged in all types of seasonal activities.

To Be a Kid, by Maya Ajmera and Jon Ivanko: Vivid photographs and a simple narrative of activities engaged in by children around the world.

Connections Between Texts

In preparing to teach children about between-text connections, think about the numerous ways in which any two (or more) pieces of text may relate. For example, two books may have similar *content*, be written in the same *genre*, be characterized by similar *writing styles*, make use of similar *text features*, or be created by the *same author* or *illustrator*. The Teacher Talk box lists a set of questions that can be applied to the text sets that follow and to any other text sets you may create. The graphic organizers featured in Figures 4–18, 4–19, and 4–20 may also be useful.

Teacher Talk: Questions for Between-Text Connections

- What is similar about the content of these texts?
- What is similar about the characters or personalities in these texts?
- What techniques do different authors use to create engaging characters?
- What is similar about the settings in these texts?
- What is similar about the themes in these texts?
- These texts are written in the same genre. Both are (folktales, tall tales, biographies, autobiographies, poems, weather reports,

advertisements, invitations). What similarities do you notice in the way they are organized?

- These books have similar problem-resolution sequences. What are the similarities?
- These authors have similar writing styles. What similarities do you notice?
- These illustrators use similar media. What are the characteristics of these media?
- These books make use of some of the same text features. What similarities do you notice? Is one way of organizing the features more helpful for you than the other?
- These pieces were created by the same author (or illustrator). What similarities do you notice?
- How does collecting information from more than one text help you build your understandings better than if you had used just one text?

In supporting children's awareness of between-text connections, you support them in putting together different pieces of their understandings and building them into a synchronous new whole.

Is a Dolphin a Fish? by Melvin and Gilda Berger

Dolphin's First Day: The Story of a Bottlenose Dolphin, by Kathleen Zoehfeld

Two nonfiction books about dolphins.

The Great Kapok Tree, by Lynne Cherry

The People Who Hugged the Trees, adapted by Deborah Lee Rose

The Earth Is Painted Green, edited by Barbara Brenner

Endangered Animals, by Gallimard Jeunesse and Sylvain Perols

Four books addressing conservation of the natural environment.

The Story of Ruby Bridges, by Robert Coles

A Picture Book of Helen Keller, by David Adler

Two books about famous females in history.

The Very Hungry Caterpillar, by Eric Carle

The Very Busy Spider, by Eric Carle

Two books by author and illustrator Eric Carle.

Oh, No, Toto! **by Katrin Hyman Tchana and Louise Tchana Pami**

It Takes a Village, **by Jane Cowen-Fletcher**

Two books about adventuresome young children.

Yeh-Shen: A Cinderella Story from China, **retold by Ai-Ling Louie.**

The Golden Sandal: A Middle Eastern Cinderella Story, **by Rebecca Hickox**

Two Cinderella stories.

Stellaluna, **by Janell Cannon**

Owl Babies, **by Martin Waddell**

Two books with similar problem-resolution sequences.

Books for Teaching Children to Decide What's Important

When collecting books to model ways of deciding what's important, choose topics that relate closely to your students' curricular inquiries or their personal interests. Since what's important depends on particular readers' goals, it is critical that children have familiarity with, or at least a good interest in, the topic at hand so that substantive goals may be set.

Using text structure (nonfiction) to decide what is important

A River Ran Wild, **by Lynne Cherry**

One way to decide what is important in a text is to figure out how it is *organized* or *structured*. *A River Ran Wild* is a true, environmental history of a river that is polluted and eventually cleaned up. The author uses a time-order sequence. Using a time line with this text will help your students see how the text is organized and at the same time develop a clear picture of the river's history. As you work through the time line, focus on recording just the main ideas.

Other common nonfiction structures that can tune children in to what's important include *description, cause and effect, comparison*, and *problem resolution*. See Figure 2–4 for a set of graphic organizers that can be used to support children's exploration of these structures.

Using text structure (fiction) to decide what is important

Mrs. Katz and Tush, **by Patricia Polacco**

Mrs. Katz feels very alone after her husband dies, but eventually her loneliness is eased through her relationship with a neighboring family.

This story, as do many for young children, features key story elements: interesting *characters*, a *setting* worth paying attention to, and a *problem* with a creative *resolution*. Identifying these elements helps children to tune in to what is important in a story and capture its main ideas. To guide children in identifying key story elements, consider using a story map (see Figures 4–5, 4–6, and 4–7).

Using questions to decide what is important

All About Rattlesnakes, by Jim Arnosky

A reader's *questions* often set the stage for deciding what is important. Almost any book can be used to model this strategy. Imagine, for example, that your class is studying reptiles. You could share with your students some questions about rattlesnakes and then use *All About Rattlesnakes* to show how your questions frame your decisions about what is important.

Looking for the theme

The Gold Coin, by Alma Flor Ada

Set in Central America, *The Gold Coin* is the story of Juan, a thief who is trying to catch up with the kind old Dona Josefa so that he may steal her gold. In the beginning, Juan is pale and sickly, shriveled and bent, and without friends and relatives to make him smile, but this changes over the course of the story, as Juan discovers something important about the meaning of *richness*. Sometimes, we direct children to pay attention to certain *story elements* (often the theme) because we know it will enhance their understanding of the story. What they pay attention to determines what is important. As you read this story with children, model your ways of looking for and thinking about the theme. Other possibilities involve focusing on how a setting is described or how a character is developed.

Considering important ideas versus interesting details

> *A Picture Book of Sojourner Truth*, by David Adler: A biography of a civil rights pioneer.
> *A Picture Book of George Washington*, by David Adler: A biography of the first president of the United States.
> *A Picture Book of Simon Bolivar*, by David Adler: The story of a Venezuelan hero dedicated to freeing his country from Spanish rule.

Often, children need to listen to or read a text in order to develop understandings about the big ideas it contains. Considering the differences between *important ideas* and *interesting details* allows them to keep track of the main ideas without getting bogged down in the details. To teach this strategy with the biographies listed here, model your ways of deciding what is important by stating your particular goal. For example, you might ask, "What were _____'s major accomplishments?" As you read, show students how you focus on key events rather than listing every detail. The information you collect could be documented on an exposition web (Figure 4–9), an Ideas and Details chart (Figure 4–21), or a time line (Figure 4–22).

Books for Teaching Children to Evaluate

Evaluation is a good comprehension builder for young children because it propels them to read text deeply and to think about its content and style. Depending on your goals, almost any book can be used to teach children to evaluate.

Critiquing and establishing opinions about content

The Mary Celeste, **by Jane Yolen and Heidi Elisabet Yolen Stemple**

The *Mary Celeste* is a real ship that was found adrift at sea in 1872. Although the crew was never found, many people have theories about what happened. The book offers the information necessary for students to develop their own theories, and it explains theories that others have developed. Use this text to teach your students to *critique ideas* presented in text (to critique the theories others have offered about the ship) and to use the facts presented to *establish their own ideas and opinions*. For example, you might ask, "Which theories seem logical?" "Do they take all the facts into account?" "What is your theory?" "What factual evidence supports it?"

Critiquing and establishing opinions about language use

When the Earth Wakes, **by Ani Rucki**

Evaluate the *imagery* and *metaphoric language* of this beautifully written story. The author begins with, "When the earth wakes in spring . . . she throws off her snowy blankets, and dances with fresh, soft breezes." Use such well-crafted literature to engage with children in conversations about style. For example, ask, "What does this language mean?" "How does the author's play with language enhance her writing?" "What do you think of the way this author uses language?"

Evaluating style of presentation

All About Owls, **by Jim Arnosky**

All About Deer, **by Jim Arnosky**

Many of Jim Arnosky's books begin with a series of pages that show a life-size portrait of an animal. These pages are followed by a set of questions that help the reader understand what the text is about. Then, each book contains a narrative along with numerous illustrations. These books (and others like it) can serve as a tool for teaching children to evaluate the ways in which nonfiction authors present information. As you read, model for children your thinking about items such as those appearing in the Teacher Talk box.

Teacher Talk: Considering Presentation of Information in Nonfiction Texts

- What do you think about this book?
- What do you think about the author's choice of title? Why?
- How does the author introduce the text? How do the questions at the beginning of the book help introduce you to the text?
- Is the language clear and easy to understand? What makes it easy or hard?
- Is it easy to find information? What makes it easy or hard?
- How does the author help us understand the definitions for new words?
- Does the book contain information that you find interesting? What makes it interesting?
- Does the author make you care about the topic? How?
- Does the book contain enough information on a topic, or does the author jump around from topic to topic?
- Are the text features helpful? How do they help?

Considering author intents and viewpoints

Margaret and Margarita, Margarita y Margaret, by Lynn Reiser

She's Wearing a Dead Bird on Her Head!, by Kathryn Lasky

In *Margaret and Margarita, Margarita y Margaret*, Margaret speaks English and Margarita speaks Spanish. When they meet in the park, both assume that there is nobody to play with. But as the two girls begin to interact, they discover that they can indeed play together. Use this text to teach your students to consider *author intents and viewpoints*. Discuss, for example:

- What reasons might the author have for writing this text?
- What are her views on language?
- What are her views on making new friends?

She's Wearing a Dead Bird on Her Head! tells the story of two classic North American activists, Minna Hall and Harriet Hemenway, whose work continues to save the lives of many birds. Hall and Hemenway were early members of the Audubon Society, an organization dedicated to protecting wildlife. As you read this book with children, show them how considering author intents and viewpoints gives you new perspectives on the content:

- Why do you think the author wrote this book? Why should we think about this question?

- How do you think the author feels about birds? How do you think she feels about activism? How do you think she feels about the role of women in the early 1900s?

- Do you think that people are fairly portrayed in this book? Why? Why is this an important question?

- Who should read this book? Why?

- How do these questions help you to consider new ideas related to the text?

Evaluating ways in which books can inform the taking of civic action

Prince William, by Gloria Rand

Life in the Rainforests, by Lucy Baker

In *Prince William*, after a tanker spills oil into the waters of Prince William Sound, a girl rescues a seal pup. Because this book addresses some important social issues (helping with disasters; conservation of the natural environment), it provides a meaningful launch for evaluating the ways in which information from books can inform real-life situations such as the taking of civic actions. Students may consider questions such as the following:

- In what ways am I like the main character in the story?
- How did she make a difference in her community?
- What are some ways that children in our community can make a difference?
- What could be done to prevent disasters such as the one that occurred in Prince William Sound?

Life in the Rainforests is another book that may inform the taking of civic actions. This book provides information about the animals, people, and plants living in rain forests. Ideas for conservation are included and the author suggests writing to the government to request help for rain forest countries. This book could help students develop the necessary expertise to effectively pursue such social action.

Evaluating ways in which books can inform daily life

Amazing Grace, **by Mary Hoffman**

The Big Orange Splot, **by Daniel Pinkwater**

Books are an important medium for helping students learn to take action on social issues directly affecting their lives. *Amazing Grace* tells the story of an African American girl who is challenged by peers when she expresses her wish to be Peter Pan in the class play. *The Big Orange Splot* tells the story of Mr. Plumbean, who encourages his neighbors to celebrate difference. These books can be used to help students learn to articulate their beliefs and feelings about differences and to develop their command of the language used to openly discuss issues of difference.

Bibliography of Children's Literature

Ada, A. F. 1991. *The Gold Coin*. New York: Macmillan.

Adler, D. 1990. *A Picture Book of George Washington*. New York: Holiday House.

———. 1991. *A Picture Book of Martin Luther King, Jr.* New York: Holiday House.

———. 1992a. *A Picture Book of Helen Keller*. New York: Scott Foresman.

———. 1992b. *A Picture Book of Simon Bolivar*. New York: Holiday House.

———. 1993. *A Picture Book of Jesse Owens*. New York: Holiday House.

———. 1994. *A Picture Book of Harriet Tubman*. New York: Scholastic.

———. 1996. *A Picture Book of Sojourner Truth*. New York: Holiday House.

Ajmera, M., and J. Ivanko. 1999. *To Be a Kid*. Watertown, MA: Charlesbridge.

Alvarez, J. 2000. *The Secret Footprints*. New York: Alfred A. Knopf.

Arnold, C. 1994. *Sea Turtles*. New York: Scholastic.

Arnosky, J. 1995. *All About Owls*. New York: Scholastic.

———. 1996. *All About Deer*. New York: Scholastic.

———. 1997. *All About Rattlesnakes*. New York: Scholastic.

Avison, B. 1993. *I Wonder Why I Blink and Other Questions About My Body*. New York: Scholastic.

Baker, L. 1990. *Life in the Rainforests*. New York: Two-Can Publishing.

Baylor, B. 1994. *The Table Where Rich People Sit*. New York: Aladdin.

Berger, M., and G. Berger. 2001. *Is a Dolphin a Fish?* New York: Scholastic.

Bosak, S., with L. McGaw. 1997. *Something to Remember Me By*. New York: Scholastic.

Bradby, M. 1995. *More Than Anything Else*. New York: Orchard.

Brenner, B. (editor). 1994. *The Earth Is Painted Green*. New York: Scholastic.

Brett, J. 1999. *Gingerbread Baby*. New York: G. P. Putnam's Sons.

Brooks, F. 1990. *Protecting Endangered Species*. London: Usborne.

Bruchac, J. 2000. *Crazy Horse's Vision*. New York: Lee and Low.

Bruchac, J., and T. Locker. 1995. *The Earth Under Sky Bear's Feet: Native American Poems of the Land*. New York: Philomel.

Bruchac, J., and J. London. 1992. *Thirteen Moons on Turtle's Back: A Native American Year of Moons*. New York: Philomel.

Bunting, E. 1996. *Train to Somewhere*. New York: Clarion.

———. 1998. *So Far from the Sea*. New York: Clarion.

Cannon, J. 1993. *Stellaluna*. New York: Harcourt Brace.

Carle, E. 1969. *The Very Hungry Caterpillar*. New York: Philomel.

———. 1984. *The Very Busy Spider*. New York: Putnam.

Cherry, L. 1990. *The Great Kapok Tree*. New York: Harcourt Brace and Co.

———. 1992. *A River Ran Wild*. Orlando, FL: Harcourt Brace.

Cole, J. 1995. *Magic School Bus: Inside Ralphie: A Book About Germs*. New York: Scholastic.

Coles, R. 1995. *The Story of Ruby Bridges*. New York: Scholastic.

Cooney, B. 1999. *Eleanor*. New York: Puffin.

Cowcher, H. 1988. *Rain Forest*. New York: Farrar Straus and Giroux.

Cowen-Fletcher, J. 1994. *It Takes a Village*. New York: Scholastic.

Cunningham, A. 1993. *Rainforest Wildlife*. New York: Scholastic.

Darling, K. 1996. *Rain Forest Babies*. New York: Walker.

———. 1997. *Desert Babies*. New York: Walker.

DePaola, T. 2001. *26 Fairmount Avenue*. New York: Puffin.

Dorros, A. 1991. *Abuela*. New York: Dutton.

———. 1997. *A Tree Is Growing*. New York: Scholastic.

Ehlert, L. 1991. *Red Leaf, Yellow Leaf*. Orlando, FL: Harcourt Brace.

Fox, M. 1994. *Tough Boris*. New York: Harcourt Brace.

Galdone, P. 1973. *The Three Billy Goats Gruff*. New York: Clarion.

―――. 1994. *The Three Little Pigs*. New York: Clarion.

George, K. O. 1997. *The Great Frog Race and Other Poems*. New
York: Houghton Mifflin.

Gibbons, G. 1990. *Weather Words*. New York: Holiday House.

―――. 2001. *Apples*. New York: Holiday House.

Giblin, J. C. 1998. *George Washington: A Picture Book Biography*. New
York: Scholastic.

Ginsburg, M. 1988. *The Chick and the Duckling*. New York: Aladdin.

Gomi, T. 1984. *Coco Can't Wait*. New York: William Morrow.

Grifalconi, A. 1990. *Osa's Pride*. New York: Little, Brown, and Co.

―――. 1995. *The Lion's Whiskers*. New York: Scholastic.

Grimes, N. 1984. *Meet Danitra Brown*. New York: Lothrop, Lee,
and Shepard.

Hall, Z. 1996. *The Apple Pie Tree*. New York: Scholastic.

Hawes, J. 1968. *Why Frogs Are Wet*. New York: HarperCollins.

Heller, R. 1981. *Chickens Aren't the Only Ones*. New York: Putnam.

―――. 1983. *The Reason for a Flower*. New York: Putnam.

Henkes, K. 1991. *Chrysanthemum*. New York: Greenwillow.

―――. 1996. *Lilly's Purple Plastic Purse*. New York: Greenwillow.

Hesse, K. 1999. *Come On, Rain!* New York: Scholastic.

Hickox, R. 1999. *The Golden Sandal: A Middle Eastern Cinderella
Story*. New York: Holiday House.

Himmelman, J. 1990. *Ibis: A True Whale Story*. New York:
Scholastic.

Hoberman, M. 1998. *The Seven Silly Eaters*. New York: Harcourt.

Hoffman, M. 1991. *Amazing Grace*. New York: Dial.

―――. 1995. *Boundless Grace*. New York: Dial.

Hudson, W. (selected by). 1993. *Pass It On: African American Poetry
for Children*. New York: Scholastic.

Isaacs, A. 1994. *Swamp Angel*. New York: Dutton.

Jeunesse, G., and S. Perols. 1995. *Endangered Animals*. New York:
Scholastic.

Johnson, A. 1989. *Tell Me a Story, Mama*. New York: Trumpet Club.

Keats, E. 1967. *Peter's Chair*. New York: Viking.

Kellogg, S. 1988. *Johnny Appleseed*. New York: William Morrow
and Co.

———. 1999. *Sally Ann Thunder Ann Whirlwind Crockett*. New York: Mulberry.

Kent, J. 1987. *The Fat Cat*. New York: Scholastic.

Kerley, B. 2001. *The Dinosaurs of Waterhouse Hawkins*. New York: Scholastic.

Lamm, D. 1997. *Sea Lion Roars*. Soundprints Corp Audio.

Lasky, K. 1995. *She's Wearing a Dead Bird on Her Head!* New York: Hyperion.

Lester, J. 1999. *John Henry*. London: Puffin.

Lind, A. 1994. *Black Bear Cub*. Norwalk, CT: Trudy Corp.

Lionni, L. 1985. *It's Mine!* New York: Alfred A. Knopf.

Lofts, P. (retold and illustrated by). 1983. *How the Birds Got Their Colours: An Aboriginal Story*. San Diego: Slawson Communications.

Louie, A. 1982. *Yeh-Shen: A Cinderella Story from China*. New York: Putnam.

Maass, R. 1992. *When Autumn Comes*. New York: Henry Holt and Co.

———. 1993. *When Winter Comes*. New York: Henry Holt and Co.

———. 1996a. *When Spring Comes*. New York: Henry Holt and Co.

———. 1996b. *When Summer Comes*. New York: Henry Holt and Co.

Marshall, J. 1988. *Goldilocks and the Three Bears*. New York: Dial.

Martin, R. 1992. *The Rough-Face Girl*. New York: Putnam and Grosset.

Marzollo, J. 1993. *Happy Birthday, Martin Luther King*. New York: Scholastic.

———. 1998. *How Kids Grow*. New York: Scholastic.

McDermott, G. 2001. *Raven: A Trickster Tale from the Pacific Northwest*. New York: Harcourt.

McMillan, B. 1994. *Sense Suspense*. New York: Scholastic.

Mora, P. 1998. *This Big Sky*. New York: Scholastic.

Paterson, K. 1990. *The Tale of the Mandarin Ducks*. New York: Lodestar.

Phillips, M. 1985. *The Sign in Mendel's Window*. New York: Macmillan.

Pinkney, S. 2000. *Shades of Black: A Celebration of Our Children*. New York: Scholastic.

Pinkwater, D. 1977. *The Big Orange Splot*. New York: Scholastic.

Polacco, P. 1992. *Mrs. Katz and Tush*. New York: Bantam.

Rand, G. 1992. *Prince William*. New York: Henry Holt and Co.

Rappoport, D. 2001. *Martin's Big Words*. New York: Hyperion.

Reiser, L. 1993. *Margaret and Margarita, Margarita y Margaret*. New York: Greenwillow.

Roop, C., and P. Roop. 2001. *Escape from the Ice*. New York: Scholastic.

Rose, D. (adapted by). 1990. *The People Who Hugged the Trees*. Niwot, CO: Roberts Rinehart.

Royston, A. 1991. *What's Inside? My Body*. New York: Scholastic.

Rucki, A. *When the Earth Wakes*. 1998. New York: Scholastic.

Schreiber, A. 1994. *Log Hotel*. New York: Scholastic.

Schroeder, A. 1996. *Minty: A Story of Young Harriet Tubman*. New York: Dial.

Scieska, J. 1989. *The True Story of the 3 Little Pigs!* New York: Penguin.

Serventy, V. 1983. *Penguin*. New York: Scholastic.

Shannon, D. 1998. *No, David!* New York: Scholastic.

———. 1999. *David Goes to School*. New York: Blue Sky.

Sherrow, V. 2001. *Titanic*. New York: Scholastic.

Shpakow, T. 1991. *On the Way to Christmas*. New York: Random House.

Simon, S. 1995. *Sharks*. New York: HarperTrophy.

Soto, G. 1993. *Too Many Tamales*. New York: Putnam and Grossett.

Sowler, S. 1992. *Amazing Animal Disguises*. New York: Alfred A. Knopf.

Steptoe, J. 1987. *Mufaro's Beautiful Daughters*. New York: William Morrow and Co.

Tchana, K. H., and L. T. Pani. 1997. *Oh, No, Toto!* New York: Scholastic.

Turkle, B. 1992. *Deep in the Forest*. New York: Dutton.

Vogt, G. 2001. *Solar System*. New York: Scholastic.

Waddell, M. 1992. *Owl Babies*. Cambridge, MA: Candlewick.

Wells, R. 1997. *McDuff Moves In*. New York: Hyperion.

———. 1998. *Yoko*. New York: Hyperion.

Widman, C. 1992. *The Lemon Drop Jar*. New York: Simon and Schuster.

Winter, J. 1992. *Follow the Drinking Gourd*. New York: Knopf.

Woodson, J. 2001. *The Other Side*. New York: Putnam.

Yee, P. 1992. *Roses Sing on New Snow*. New York: Macmillan.

Yolen, J. 1987. *Owl Moon*. New York: Philomel.

Yolen, J., and H. E. Y. Stemple. 2002. *The Mary Celeste*. New York: Aladdin.

Young, E. 1989. *Lon Po Po: A Red Riding Hood Story from China*. New York: Philomel.

Younger, B. 1998. *Purple Mountain Majesties*. New York: Dutton.

Zoehfeld, K. 1994. *Dolphin's First Day: The Story of a Bottlenose Dolphin*. Norwalk, CT: Trudy Corp.

References

Allington, R. 2002. "What I've Learned About Effective Reading Instruction from a Decade of Studying Exemplary Elementary Classroom Teachers." *Phi Delta Kappan* 83 (10): 740–47.

Beck, I., M. McKeown, R. Hamilton, and L. Kucan. 1997. *Questioning the Author.* Newark, DE: International Reading Association.

Berk, L., and A. Winsler. 1995. *Scaffolding Children's Learning: Vygotsky and Early Childhood Education.* Washington, DC: National Association for the Education of Young Children.

Bomer, R. 1998. "Transactional Heat and Light: More Explicit Literacy Learning." *Language Arts* 76 (1): 11–18.

Cambourne, B. 2002. "Conditions for Literacy Learning." *The Reading Teacher* 55 (8): 758–62.

Clay, M. 1985. *The Early Detection of Reading Difficulties.* 3d ed. Portsmouth, NH: Heinemann.

Cullinan, B., and L. Galda. 1998. *Literature and the Child.* 4th ed. New York: Harcourt Brace.

Griffin, M. 2002. "Why Don't You Use Your Finger? Paired Reading in First Grade." *The Reading Teacher* 55 (8): 766–74.

Houck, P. 1997. "Lessons from an Exhibition: Reflections of an Art Educator." In *First Steps Toward Teaching the Reggio Way,* ed. J. Hendrick, 26–40. Upper Saddle River, NJ: Prentice-Hall.

Ibbotson, R. 2002. "Building the Future from the Past." *Investment Forum* 6 (2): 10, 12.

Keene, E., and S. Zimmerman. 1997. *Mosaic of Thought.* Portsmouth, NH: Heinemann.

Krueger, E., and B. Braun. 1998/1999. "Books and Buddies: Peers Tutoring Peers." *The Reading Teacher* 52 (4): 410–14.

Ogle, D. 1986. "KWL: A Teaching Model That Develops Active Reading of Expository Text." *The Reading Teacher* 32: 564–70.

Owocki, G., and Y. Goodman. 2002. *Kidwatching: Documenting Children's Literacy Development*. Portsmouth, NH: Heinemann.

Pressley, Michael. 2001. "Comprehension Instruction: What Makes Sense Now, What Might Make Sense Soon." *Reading Online* 5 (2).

Raphael, T. 1986. "Teaching Question-Answer Relationships, Revisited." *The Reading Teacher* 39 (6): 516–22.

Rosenblatt, L. 1978. *The Reader, the Text, the Poem: The Transactional Theory of Literary Work*. Carbondale, IL: Southern Illinois University Press.

———. 1991. "The Reading Transaction: What For?" In *Literacy in Process*, ed. B. M. Power and R. Hubbard, 114–27. Portsmouth, NH: Heinemann.

Schultz, C. 2000. *How Partner Reading Fosters Literacy Development in First Grade Students*. Action Research Project, Saginaw Valley State University, University Center, Michigan.

Short, K., J. Harste, and C. Burke. 1996. *Creating Classrooms for Authors and Inquirers*. Portsmouth, NH: Heinemann.

Taberski, S. 2000. *On Solid Ground*. Portsmouth, NH: Heinemann.

Villaume, S., and E. Brabham. 2002. "Comprehension Instruction: Beyond Strategies." *The Reading Teacher* 55 (7): 672–75.

Vygotsky, L. S. 1978. "Mind in Society: The Development of Higher Psychological Processes." Ed. and trans. by M. Cole, V. John-Steiner, S. Scribner, and E. Souberman. Cambridge, MA: Harvard University Press.

Walczyk, J. J. 2000. "The Interplay Between Automatic and Control Processes in Reading." *Reading Research Quarterly* 35 (4): 554–66.

Wilde, S. 2000. *Miscue Analysis Made Easy: Identifying and Building on Student Strengths*. Portsmouth, NH: Heinemann.

Wood, D., J. Bruner, and G. Ross. 1976. "The Role of Tutoring in Problem Solving." *Journal of Child Psychology and Psychiatry* 17: 89–100.

Index